JOHN AUSTIN

Unquestioned Brilliance

Navigating a Fundamental Leadership Trap

FISHER BALDWIN PRESS | STATE COLLEGE, PENNSYLVANIA

Copyright © 2015 by John Austin
Published by Fisher Baldwin Press
Book design by Matthew Williams

Library of Congress Cataloging-in-Publication Data
Austin, John
Unquestioned Brilliance: navigating a fundamental leadership trap/John Austin
     p.   cm.
Includes bibliographical references.
Library of Congress Catalog Control Number: 2015913499
ISBN: 0996703705
ISBN 13: 978-0-9967037-0-3

Contents

Introduction

This book is intended to be practical. It was motivated by my desire to share the techniques I've developed over my years of working with leaders to help them break out of dysfunctional routines and better manage external uncertainties. For this reason I view the techniques described in this book as its core. Yes, some stories are included, but other writers are far better storytellers. The stories here are the side dish, not the main course. This book is about leadership but I believe it is useful for those who are just starting their managerial careers as well. Whether you are an experienced leader or stepping into your first managerial position, I hope this book gives you some new ways to think about leadership and develop yourself and those who work with you.

For the past decade, I've had a practical and intellectual interest in idea translation. Specifically, I've been intrigued by how new knowledge can be translated from the generalized research of social scientists into specific new actions by leaders of organizations. This book is designed as an example of this process. It is not a book about fascinating research studies, and it is not a book about war stories from my consulting experience.

Instead, this book is best viewed as my attempt to share the types of techniques I've used or developed over the years while attempting to help my clients translate social science research into their own war stories. In other words, the techniques I share in this book are all based on solid research about cognition, decision-making, strategic thinking, and organizational change. I developed them in the hope that they would help clients break through the barriers preventing them from being more effective.

Over time I came to realize there was an underlying theme driving the way I applied these techniques. That is the fundamental leadership trap outlined in chapter 1. I also discovered that clients consistently and predictably hit walls when confronted with three specific types of leadership challenges. These are the three translation challenges described in chapter 2. The techniques outlined here provide validated facilitation tools to help leaders, or prospective leaders, improve their own thinking as well as the thinking of their teams.

In all likelihood, all ten of these techniques are not right for everyone. If each reader of this book finds one technique out of the ten to be a valuable addition to his or her tool kit, I'd consider the purchase of this book to be an excellent investment. As simple as some of these techniques may seem, they are all valuable. I know they are valuable for two simple reasons: First, I have seen every one of these techniques contribute to a profound insight and problem resolution. Sometimes the simplest technique creates the most transformative idea. Second, each of these techniques, all derived from solid research, are direct attempts to translate scholarly, empirical evidence about decision-making, cognition, and social dynamics into specific tools for leading groups and organizations.

The ten techniques range from simple, quick group exercises (such as the backward-forward flip and tension tracking) to complex processes (such as uncertainty vectoring and TAP analysis) that may need the assistance of experienced facilitators. I sincerely hope that at least one of these tools will help you enable your team and organization to thrive in this uncertain world.

Unquestioned Brilliance and Leadership Challenges

Unquestioned brilliance is sneaky. Unquestioned brilliance is a leadership hindrance that emerges from your past successes. It is a fundamental leadership trap that potentially grows stronger over time. In chapter 1, I introduce this trap. Unquestioned brilliance is pervasive and in the interest of offering practical techniques to help leaders and groups overcome this trap, I narrow the focus of this book to a few specific types of challenges that all leaders face when attempting to move organizations and groups in new directions. These are the three leadership challenges described in chapter 2

Part I establishes the framework and structure for the book. In subsequent parts of the book I will present techniques for countering the natural tendency towards this fundamental trap when working through the key leadership challenges.

The Fundamental Leadership Trap

Defining Unquestioned Brilliance

Unquestioned brilliance sounds like a good idea. After all, how can brilliance be bad? But, in the context of this book, unquestioned brilliance is bad. Unquestioned brilliance is being so confident in your own intelligence and point of view that you not only fail to question your conclusions, but you may not even see the potential for other points of view or better solutions.

Unquestioned brilliance is not just overconfidence or a problem for egotistical megalomaniacs, however. I contend that unquestioned brilliance is something that every leader struggles with. This does not mean every leader is an egotistical megalomaniac; it means every leader is human. Every one of us struggles with balancing ignorance (what we don't know) with overconfidence (what we want to believe we know). The unquestioned brilliance at the center of this book is not simply arrogance. It is far more subtle and pervasive than that.

All leaders must walk a fine line between focus and conventional wisdom, between confidence in their ability and unrealistic overconfidence, and between the demands of fast action and a clear-eyed assessment of the situation. Unquestioned brilliance gets in the way of maintaining this balance. It is a fundamental leadership trap—perhaps *the* fundamental leadership trap. In this chapter, I examine the three essential variables that combine to form this trap.

Thinking about Thinking

I would like for you to guess what sport I played in college, and I will tell you a little about myself to help you guess. I am not a big man. I stand five eight, weigh approximately 140 pounds, and I went to college in the United States. Knowing just these facts about me, take a guess. You will likely agree that whatever guess you made was just that...a guess. You do not know what sport I played, so you accept the few clues, mentally fill in the gaps, and form a pattern in your mind. In this case, you have a mental model of athletes from various sports. You then simply compare my description to that mental model based on your experience. The result is your guess. Does this sound like a reasonable way to describe the thought process you just used to make your guess?

There is nothing wrong with this process. We do it all the time in our attempt to make sense of the world. We have to make guesses based on incomplete information. The mental models we use to fill the gaps in our knowledge are built over our years of experience. In all likelihood, our mental models help us more than they harm us. This relatively unconscious process, which we use every day to navigate a complex world, gets in our way only when we are unable to challenge it and become unaware of *how* we fill in the gaps in our perception. It gets in the way when the world is transforming in ways that our experience cannot predict.

The exercise of guessing what sport I played gets quite a bit more interesting if I were to give you ten minutes to think about your initial guess. If I were to do this—and not tell you anything else about myself—at the end of the ten minutes, you would likely come back more confident that your initial guess was correct. Rather than spend that ten minutes considering alternative sports or the pros and cons of your initial guess, you would likely spend that time convincing yourself that your guess was a great guess. This effect would be strengthened if you publicly stated your guess at the onset. Multiple research studies find evidence that we actively search for information that matches our expectations.[1] This occurs not just when we feel passionately about one answer but also when we have made public our initial guesses or thoughts. We've become such experts at discounting disconfirming evidence that we do it even when the stakes are low (such as when an author asks you to guess the sport he played or when you are playing trivia at a bar with your friends).[2]

By making the guess public, we have created a sense of ownership, and it turns out we are loath to change our opinion publicly, even in the case where our initial choice was clearly just a guess. Combine the desire to be seen as right with our skill at automatically filling gaps in our information with made-up details, and we have a strong tendency toward the rationalization and justification of initial guesses.

The process you just went through in trying to guess what sport I played is an illustration of a cognitive process that is one of the biggest challenges to becoming an effective leader. It is a cognitive path of least resistance. It starts with a single, rapid, often unconscious understanding of the situation and proceeds with an active effort to look for evidence that you are right, which drives toward an overconfident belief that you are correct. This cycle feeds on itself, because once you start to find evidence that you are correct, you grow even more confident in your initial framing of the situation. This cognitive path of least resistance is a relatively unconscious, reinforcing cycle that successful leaders (as shown in Figure 1-1) have learned to resist.

Once you start looking for this cognitive path of least resistance, you start to realize how much it affects leadership actions, as the examples in the following list illustrate.

- We give the benefit of the doubt to those employees we were responsible for hiring. Yet we are quick to judge, in a negative way, those employees someone else hired.
- We set our strategy based on today's world, and we are slow to acknowledge when fundamental changes in the external environment make this strategy no longer a good fit for tomorrow's world.

7

Figure 1-1 The Cognitive Path of Least Resistance.

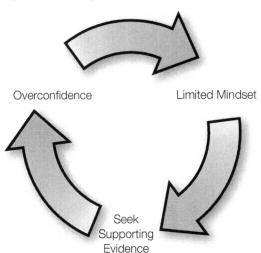

Overconfidence　　　　　　　Limited Mindset

Seek
Supporting
Evidence

- We spend significant amounts of money attempting to understand how satisfied our customers are. Yet we spend little time trying to understand why people choose not to be our customers or questioning the way we gathered data about our current customers.
- We carefully design large-scale change initiatives. Yet we do not look for, or even acknowledge, the blind spots in our plans.
- We eagerly review industry reports written by acknowledged experts. Yet we are quick to dismiss reports written by industry outsiders as ill informed.

Incidentally, I was a wrestler in college. If you were one of the few readers of this book to guess wrestling, right now you may be feeling pretty good about yourself for your successful guess. However, it was still just a guess. That is a hard reality to keep in mind whenever our guesses turn out to be correct. Correct guesses are so easily transformed into evidence of our wisdom, or brilliance, in our minds.

The intent of this book is not to suggest that these mental shortcuts are the only impediment to effective leadership. But in the process of working to avoid this cognitive path of least resistance, leaders are forced to become more aware of their environment, more mindful of how they draw conclusions, and more disciplined in their interactions with others. By starting your leadership development journey confronting how this dysfunctional dynamic plays out in your own life, you build new habits and develop the critical-thinking skills that form a foundation for virtually everything you do as a leader. The techniques described in this book will not automatically make you a great leader, but they will potentially help you navigate your team on a path that avoids this dysfunctional cycle. Starting with how we quickly and unconsciously frame our thinking, let's examine each of the three parts of the fundamental leadership trap in more detail.

Starting with Quantum Physics

Quantum physics makes no sense. Until it does, I spent many hours trying to understand the basics of quantum physics.[3] Consider the principle of wave-particle duality in quantum mechanics. Wave-particle duality is the concept that elementary entities exhibit characteristics of both particles and waves. Logically, I can understand it almost immediately, yet intuitively my mind rebels. It makes no sense. Every time I try to grasp the idea, it leads me down paths that make no sense. And then it clicks. My mind relaxes. I stop clinging so strongly to a particle-anchored framing of the world. Wave-particle duality suddenly makes sense.

At this point, an interesting realization happens. Not only can I understand the basics of wave-particle duality, but I can also see the limitation of my initial framing of quantum physics. Subsequent reading on the topic seems to fit more smoothly into my mind. This example illustrates why it is so difficult to break out of our limited frames of reference when confronting complex issues. We approach most problems within a single frame of reference, and we are quite often not aware of the frame. Once we break out of the frame, we start to see a variety of perspectives on the same situation.

Consider the classic visual-perception exercise of the image of the young woman and the old woman (Figure 1-2).[4]

When you first see this image, you tend to see one or the other (old woman or young woman). No matter how many times you have seen this image, it still takes some cognitive effort to see the

Figure 1-2 Do you see an old woman or a young woman or both?

second woman. But once you have seen both women, notice how easy it is to move back and forth between the two images. It is the first reframing that takes effort. It is the first reframing that will not happen on its own. Someone has to tell you there is a second woman in the picture—or that you need to try to stop thinking about an electron as an object (wave-particle duality). The good news is that once the initial reframing occurs, it becomes almost effortless to switch among multiple frames.

Eureka!

Think back on a moment in your life when you simply could not understand something, and then suddenly it all clicked for you. Understanding a complex topic does not always emerge gradually; it is often sudden. Much like those Magic Eye books from the 1990s in which 3-D images would suddenly jump out of the page at you when you looked at the 2-D picture just the right way, insight often comes from a sudden reconfiguring of the situation. Eureka!

Most innovations involve at least one eureka moment—the instant when people realize they have found their way to something new, exciting, and potentially valuable.[5] It is the breakthrough. The eureka moment is glamorized in stories of innovation and recounted over and over. It is the moment that becomes part of the company lore. Breakthroughs are exciting to experience, and these moments create momentum and commitment. Strategic leaders need to be able to recognize them when they occur and create the context for enabling such moments.

The focus on the breakthrough moment does have a downside. It can create unrealistic expectations about implementation, impatience with the slow pace of behavior change, and confusion on the part of those who were not part of the eureka moment. The translation of the breakthrough into organizational action is the core activity of the second translation moment described in chapter 2. The insight itself is not that big of a deal; rather, it is what the leader does with it that matters.

Though the breakthrough is not the only part, or even the hardest part, of the innovation process, it is the key trigger that initiates and sets the direction. Finding the first reframing of the issue, that eureka moment, is worth aspiring toward for several reasons:

- The breakthrough infuses the process with energy. Organizational change and innovation are hard to pull off. All the tendencies within an organizational structure are in the direction of stability and routine. The breakthrough moment is exciting and generates momentum and enthusiasm. The value of this injection of positive energy and emotion cannot be overstated.
- The breakthrough potentially creates awe. We don't talk much about awe, but perhaps we should. Melanie Rudd, Kathleen Vohs, and Jennifer Aaker studied how awe influences decision-making and well-being. They define *awe* roughly as a moment that involves perceptual vastness or the sense that something is "big." Awe also prompts observers to rethink their views of the world in some key way. Awe can focus people on the present and expand their perception of time available.[6] Given that many executives claim they do not have time for strategic thinking and innovation exercises, this expanding of the perception of time may be the most important outcome of a truly awesome eureka moment. Of course, we have to admit that not every innovation inspires awe, but the potential is there.

11

- The breakthrough generates commitment. Participants involved in a strategic decision grow more committed to the decision if it includes innovative ideas. Early in my career, I found this to be the case when studying merchandising teams in a consumer products company.[7] My work facilitating strategic decisions has reinforced this point. An idea champion or, ideally, multiple champions emerge from the eureka moment, and passionate champions can make a difference when working to get the resources needed to test ideas.
- The breakthrough clarifies a sense of purpose. The eureka moment often involves shifting mindsets around the organizational purpose. The insight reveals hidden value and may even answer the questions, "How are we making the world a better place?" or "Why does our organization matter?" The purposeful focus on these questions, combined with the positive answer of the innovation, can create a recommitment to the organization. I have seen these moments create palpable feelings of pride and purpose.

Reframing often happens suddenly. When it does, it can create momentum, commitment, and pride. Leaders need to look for and encourage these frame-breaking moments. To create a realistic eureka moment, leaders must help their groups work through three tasks:

1. Breaking out of taken-for-granted, shared frames and questioning organization or industry assumptions
2. Creating a new understanding of future possibilities and current strategies
3. Preparing a plan to act on the insight

While limited frames create problems from idea generation to execution, breaking out of frames is the primary way we create new insight in organizations. The tools for helping leaders navigate the task of generating strategic options or creating innovative ideas are all built around a goal of breaking out of limited and taken-for-granted mindsets.

Figure 1-3 The Lucky Iron Fish

The Lucky Iron Fish Project:
The Simplicity of a Frame-Breaking Solution

Iron deficiency is a serious problem in many developing countries. Estimates vary widely, but iron deficiency affects between 20 percent and 50 percent of the world's population.[8] In children, such deficiency leads to a range of developmental issues, including lethargy, insufficient weight gain, more frequent respiratory and intestinal infections, and impaired behavioral and cognitive skills.

The case of Dr. Christopher Charles and the Lucky Iron Fish illustrates the type of solution that can emerge from frame breaking. Dr. Charles was studying anemia in rural Cambodia. Many families could not afford to eat iron-rich food and were unable to afford iron supplements or cast-iron pots. Dr. Charles distributed small iron blocks to families and instructed them to place the blocks in the water as they boiled it for their rice. But he found that the local women could not be convinced to put something as unappealing as a block of iron into their cooking pots.

Dr. Charles, along with Gavin Armstrong, had the insight that the Cambodian women may be more likely to put something in their cooking pots if it was tied to a symbol of good luck. He learned of a fish, called a try kantrop, that was eaten locally and viewed as a sign of good luck.[9] Thus was born the Lucky Iron Fish Project. The community was far more enthusiastic about putting this symbol of good luck into their cooking pots (see Figure 1-3), and within a year, community anemia plummeted. In fact, Gavin Armstrong, CEO of the Lucky Iron Fish Project, and his team report that use of the Lucky Iron Fish is currently at 92 percent, leading to significant reduction in anemia rates.[10]

We sometimes assume frame breaking needs to be earth-shattering. In fact, most innovations are simply a case of taking the perspective of someone else and making connections between two somewhat unrelated pieces of information. Dr. Charles stepped into the shoes of the local Cambodian women and reframed the question in terms of cooking aesthetics rather than in terms of public health.

Locked-In Mindsets and Leadership

Leaders counter limited frames by cultivating two skills: frame breaking and frame triggering.[11] Frame breaking is challenging existing frames to create new insights and draw from multiple perspectives. Frame triggering is activating alternative frames in the minds of others. Reframing takes effort and will not happen on its own. The cognitively lazy approach is to accept what is initially understood as a given. People will almost always choose the cognitively lazy approach unless challenged in some manner (for example, I will not see the old woman in the picture unless I am told she is there). Leaders can use the techniques in this book to break frames to generate insight and to trigger frames in others that enable action. Finally, resilient leaders use knowledge of framing effects to embed actions and mindsets into the routines of the organization's culture.

Unfortunately, locked-in mindsets are not the end of the fundamental leadership trap. Left to our well-honed, pattern-seeking tendencies, we will begin paying attention to those parts of our environment that fit our frames. Just as significant, we will ignore or downplay those parts of our environment that do not fit our frame. Not only is our brilliance unquestioned, it is inappropriately reinforced by our search for evidence. In the next section, we examine this search for confirming evidence.

The Confirmation Bias

Human understanding when it has once adopted an opinion...draws all things else to support and agree with it. And though there be a

Unquestioned Brilliance and Leadership Challenges

greater number and weight of instances to be found on the other side, yet these it either neglects or despises, or else by some distinction sets aside or rejects.

—Francis Bacon, *Novum Organum*

We make all of our plans at the moment we know the least about the world. It is only after we set our plans in motion that we really begin to understand the situation. It is at that moment we start to get information about how well our plans actually fit and interact with a complex world. Yet we have such confidence in our plans, in spite of the observation that more often than not our plans do not work as intended. Is it really a surprise when sales targets for 2016 that we set in August 2015 didn't play out as expected, much like those targets we set in 2015, 2014, and 2013? Occasionally we seem to get it right, but that's the exception more than the rule.

Does this sound familiar to you? In my conversations with planners, most readily accept that their plans do not generally play out as expected. Yet most also admit to me that they always have significant confidence in those plans when they make them. At the end of the day, there is really only one thing you can say with confidence about any long-term plan: it is wrong. You just don't know what part of it is wrong yet. This is not to say that planning is a useless process. A good strategic plan provides focus and creates clarity around organizational priorities. A well-run organization needs to devote resources to plans. What planning doesn't do well is predict the future.

Strategic planning is an excellent context in which to highlight the risk of confirmation bias, or the tendency to search for and overvalue information that validates a currently held position or belief. Confirmation bias is particularly dangerous for leaders when it is combined with limited frames and overconfidence. A strategic planning process provides a wonderful breeding ground for all three of these dysfunctions. The final strategic plan creates the frame of reference as a simplified understanding of the future environment. But, as is the case with any simplification of a complex system, a strategic plan has blind spots. Because of the work that's gone into building the strategic plan, managers and leaders tend to have a significant degree of confidence that they've done a good job and that they've created a plan that will work well for them. Now, all that is left is executing the plan and tracking progress toward the goals. And this is the moment the confirmation bias rears its ugly head.

At the end of the designated period, we will know whether or not we hit our targets. But prior to that, all we can do is track progress toward our targets, and progress is far more ambiguous. Managers have many choices of what data to track and, more important, how to weigh the importance of data. The plan created a pattern of how we expect the year to play out. Our focus of attention is naturally drawn to the data that fit that pattern. At the same time, we discount the data that do not fit the pattern. This results in a common pattern that I see play out during an organization's annual cycle.

During the first quarter, organizations feel as if they are on track with their plan. Even if they are not reaching their numbers, they find multiple rationalizations to explain the slow start, and leaders convince one another that their plan is still a good one. Because the end result is most ambiguous during the first quarter, this is perhaps the time when the confirmation bias plays the greatest role.

By second quarter, pressure builds to explain discrepancies between reality and the plan. This may be a time of some soul-searching within the organization, but generally the argument that wins out is that the plan is still attainable. Once again, numerous data sources are provided to support this argument.

In the third quarter, reality sets in, and most organizations start to adjust their plans to align with reality. Interestingly, at this moment, when the organization is most likely to admit that the plan from the previous year was not as accurate as they would've hoped, the leaders are currently immersed in planning for the next year. More often than not, they are following the very same process that led to the inaccurate projections for the current year.

The fourth quarter is when the leaders confront the reality. You would think this would be an excellent time to learn from the discrepancy, but, of course, this is difficult because the planning for the next year has ready been completed, and a significant focus of the organization is already working on the targets for the new year.

I use the example of planning to illustrate just one of the ways that confirmation bias can harm us. A number of studies have shown that our desire to find evidence that we are right is deeply embedded in so much of what we do.[12] It is easy to tell people to just watch out for this. I do this when I say things like, "Look for evidence that you're wrong." Such advice makes it seem like it is so easy to fix. But the overwhelming evidence from studies of decision-making and cognitive processing suggests that this bias happens to us automatically. It is not a conscious choice that we make. Leaders cannot just rely on developing a personal discipline of challenging their own expectations of success. Rather, a more sustainable approach to correcting the confirmation bias is to adopt some tools and techniques that will remind us to challenge our preconceived notions and our discounting of negative information.

Limited mindsets and our desire to seek supporting evidence put us well on our way toward unquestioned brilliance. These dynamics create the unquestioned nature of it. The final dynamic, overconfidence, is responsible for our sense of brilliance. In the next section, we examine this.

Overconfidence

Overconfident professionals sincerely believe they have expertise, act as experts and look like experts. You will have to struggle to remind yourself that they may be in the grip of an illusion.
—Daniel Kahneman, *Thinking, Fast and Slow*

Overconfidence contributes to the difficulty we often have of breaking out of our initial framing of a situation. Overconfidence is a pervasive bias that makes the examination of multiple perspectives not just difficult but personally threatening to our self-identity. It leads people to believe they know more than they really know, to downplay the possibility of failure, and to reject alternate perspectives as simply misinformed.[13] It is difficult for leaders to look for new mindsets when they are convinced their current framing of the world is correct. It becomes even more difficult if leaders have already invested part of their reputation in the previous choices that led to the current shared perspective.[14] The curiosity needed to create a new mindset emerges from a recognition that leaders do not know everything they need to know about the situation.

The distinction between self-assurance and overconfidence is vital. These two states are often confused. We teach people to speak confidently. We train people to not start off their statements by saying, "I don't know." But there is a difference between appropriate confidence and overconfidence. Self-assurance and appropriate confidence are based on knowledge and understanding. Overconfidence is based on delusion and inaccurate assessments.

We frequently encounter two types of overconfidence in our interactions with others: social overconfidence, or pretending to be more confident about what we are saying than we actually feel; and cognitive overconfidence, or thinking we know more than we actually do. Obviously, these are two quite different dynamics, but from a practical point of view, both lead to the same types of outcomes and can cause the same dysfunctions within organizations. Since it is difficult to assess what other people actually know, we must rely on how they state their opinions. Whether overconfidence emerges from their desire to look intelligent or from a belief that they really are more intelligent, it presents itself to others in the same manner.

Social overconfidence is a result of our environment. The extent to which we are at risk of social overconfidence depends on our training, profession, organizational culture, national culture, and, of course, our personality. Certain professions lend themselves to overconfidence in communication, and the one that immediately comes to mind is the physician.[15] The job of the physician is to give an answer to an ill-defined problem. Patients are not satisfied if doctors cannot give direct answers, so significant external pressure is exerted on physicians. In addition, physicians often find themselves at the top of an organizational hierarchy, which puts additional pressure on them to feel as if they should have answers. This type of environment creates a perfect storm for social overconfidence. Individual physicians are not necessarily automatically overconfident, but they do work in an environment that encourages overconfidence.

In general, the more your job consists of providing exact answers and maintaining a high level of competence, the greater your risk for falling into the trap of continually communicating that you know more than you actually know. Leaders fall into this trap, just like anyone else. In fact, leaders may be more at risk because they certainly feel personal pressure to be viewed as competent. Given that leaders set the direction of the organization, it is in an organization's best interest to ensure their leaders do not cross the line between self-assurance and overconfidence.

In addition to our profession, the way we are conditioned to communicate further encourages overconfidence. From the time when we first gave presentations in front of our classes or wrote papers in school, we have been taught to underemphasize uncertainty and focus on provable "facts." While the focus on facts is most certainly an important element in critical thinking, this communication pattern of debate trains us to make statements in a factual manner, even if they are shrouded in uncertainty. The end result of this is when we hear speakers publicly discuss their uncertainty when giving their opinion, and we tend to, at least slightly, discount their knowledge. This routine translation from uncertainty into factual statement is so ingrained in our style of communication that we rarely question it.

The frequent confusion and disconnect between scientific research and public policy debates often hinge on the automatic nature of this translation. A good example of this translation is seen in weather forecasting. Meteorology is a deeply scientific field with language based on probabilities and uncertainty. As a general rule, meteorologists do not predict the weather. Rather, they work to generate a set of realistic probabilities of how the numerous variables in a highly complex system will interact to generate a certain outcome. Contrast that with the manner in which most of us consume our weather forecasts. What we want to know are the facts, not the probabilities. So some poor meteorologist is left with the unenviable job of translating meteorological models, based on uncertainties, into statements of fact that will drive the decision-making for thousands of people. We want to know the exact temperature, the time—down to the minute—that rain will start and stop, how many inches of snow will fall, and exactly how slippery the roads will be during our commutes into work. We will make specific decisions about our day based on these statements. The inevitable result of this system is frustration or anger when the forecasts do not play out as we had been led to believe.

An interesting study by Susan Joslyn and Jared LeClerc illustrates how this specific translation of uncertainty into certainty can lead to inferior decision-making.[16] They studied false alarms in weather-related decision-making. Participants were given temperature data as well as advice on whether to apply salt to the local roads. A false alarm occurred when the temperature remained above freezing, but the decision tool recommended salting the roads. The study found that the overall quality of decisions made went down in the trials where the false-alarm rate was significantly above or below average. Unfortunately, simply reducing the false-alarm rate did not significantly increase decision quality.

What did increase decision quality was the addition of an uncertainty estimate in the data shared with the decision-makers. Essentially, by bringing some of the uncertainty back into the conversation, by untranslating, decision quality was improved.[17] This dynamic of finding ways to reintroduce uncertainty into decision processes, but doing so in a way that does not paralyze the decision-makers, is a common theme connecting the techniques described in this book.

Cognitive overconfidence is perhaps more challenging than social overconfidence. In the case of cognitive overconfidence, we don't even recognize the problem. Unless we get feedback, we happily go on believing that we know more than we actually know. Studies of overconfidence have found evidence that it exists in individuals of all ages at all levels of expertise and in nations across the world.[18] We overestimate our expertise even in those areas in which we are relatively expert. This happens because fields of expertise evolve, and often our knowledge of those fields does not keep pace.

Imagine you were a world-class expert in some field ten years ago. You had just emerged from graduate school, and, by any measure, you could be considered an expert in your given field. Over the next ten years, that field of knowledge continued to expand. During that same time, you spent your time doing other things: managing budgets, taking up a hobby, recruiting people, and so on. In other words, as the field has evolved, your expertise has become dated. To a certain extent you understand that, and your perception of your expertise has gone down. The difficulty is that your perception of your own expertise degrades at a slower rate than your actual expertise. Over time, a gap emerges between what you know and what you think you know.

This gap can be explained by several factors. First, it is likely that you still know more about this topic than most of the people you work with. You're no longer comparing yourself to world experts to assess your own expertise, but rather you are comparing yourself to other people within your organization. Therefore, you do not get feedback that your knowledge is less than you think it is. Second, you identify as an expert. This becomes part of how you see yourself; therefore, it is no longer something that is questioned.

When I was a professor, I had several occasions in which a student would be in my office after they'd earned a poor grade on one of my assignments, and they would blurt out, "But I am an A student," as if being an A student was a personality trait rather than something they earned every semester.[19] As humorous as that is, we all struggle with the same problem once we self-identify as an expert. It is too easy to forget that being an expert is something that we earn and must work to maintain rather than just something that we are.

Avoiding Three Overconfidence Traps
Trap Number One: We Don't Know What We Don't Know
Leaders need to be constantly vigilant against the temptation to believe their understanding goes beyond their actual area of expertise. I've often encountered people who can talk for thirty minutes explaining how complex their industry is or how it takes years of experience to understand their area of expertise. Yet these same people are quick to pass judgment or to espouse a "common sense" solution to a complex problem that is not within their area of expertise. These same people seem incredulous that others do not see what seems like such an obvious solution to them. In other words, these individuals see complexity in the areas in which they are experts but see only simplicity in the areas in which they are not. Here are some common examples of this:

21

- The equities analyst assessing the difficulty of major company mergers
- The business executive discussing government dysfunction
- The new member of the House of Representatives, who was a local politician or local business owner prior to their election, stating an opinion on geopolitical instability as if it should be obvious
- The television pundit on practically any issue[20]

It is tempting to let our intelligence or our experience and success in one field of knowledge cloud our judgment about what we don't know. Physicians, business executives, and university professors certainly are at higher risk of falling into this trap than are many other people simply because they find themselves in roles in which people expect them to be the most knowledgeable person in the room. This is not to say that every physician, business executive, and university professor falls into this trap, only that they are in a professional setting that puts them at risk. Leaders need to be mindful of this risk in their own context.

There is an old adage that states that successful leaders surround themselves with people who are smarter than they are. I would add that successful leaders also recognize and acknowledge that those people around them are smarter than they are. Assuming someone else in the room has a better answer than you do is not a bad habit to cultivate. Such an assumption changes the default behavior of the leader from trying to declare the correct answer to trying to discover who has the best answer and skillfully coaxing that answer out of them.

Trap Number Two: We Forget What We Used to Not Know
In the United States, this trap is often called "Monday morning quarterbacking," in reference to American football, and refers to the tendency to criticize the actions of the athletes playing in the Sunday games. Sports fans, and I readily admit to doing this many times, criticize the foolish decisions made by the athletes. Of course, if we stopped to think about this, most of us will readily admit that the play is now classified as foolish only because it did not work. We forget that the quarterback did not know that the

play would not work when he did it. More important, we forget that we did not know that the play would fail. In reality, if the play had succeeded, on Monday morning we would likely be singing the praises of that same player whom we now criticize.

This difficulty in remembering that we did not have the knowledge in the past that we have now has been well documented in numerous studies.[21] This is one reason why social scientists and criminal investigators have learned to be careful in their reliance on eyewitness accounts. Retrospective sense making is notoriously poor. We naturally fill in the gaps in our memories with "facts" that we just assume must have happened. In essence, we create false memories that fill out the pattern and explain what we saw.

Forgetting what we did not know hinders the ability to assess projects and complete performance reviews. If left unchallenged, it is far too easy for leaders to conclude that they would have done things differently than the person they are assessing. Obviously, this conclusion is more likely to happen when things do not go well. The result of this trap is that leaders may be too quick to place blame. This trap also conveniently reinforces the leaders' own perception of competence. Thus, overconfidence comes not just from reliving your own successes but also from reliving the failures of others and convincing yourself that you would have acted differently.

Trap Number Three: Our Success Reinforces Our Overconfidence
When I was a faculty member at the Penn State School of Business, one of my tasks was to teach MBA students to be better team leaders. I learned rather quickly that few students enroll in MBA programs to become better team leaders. A vast majority of incoming MBA students are quite convinced they are already excellent team leaders. In fact, my highly unscientific observation is that a far higher percentage of incoming MBA students believe they are great team leaders than do the experienced senior executives I've had the pleasure to work with since leaving my faculty position.

Why is this the case? What is it about the life experience of incoming MBA students that leads them to such a high degree of overconfidence in regard to their ability as team leaders? I believe it is their experience. More to the point, it is their success. Many of these students have experienced primarily successes in their previous teams. Those students accepted into a leading MBA program have perhaps had many experiences in which they were the smartest person on their team. For many of them, the MBA experience will be the first time in their professional lives that they are placed with a team of peers who are all as intelligent as they are. Their past success quite logically leads to a current sense of overconfidence. The senior executives I've worked with have been exposed to a greater number of accomplished and more experienced individuals. Their successes are perhaps tempered by a more realistic understanding of the knowledge that other people bring to the table.

A humorous illustration of the tendency to assume success is a shirt that a friend of mine recently showed me. The shirt reads, "I went to Johns Hopkins University/Let's save time and just assume I am right." You can surely find the same shirt being sold at any other elite university in place of Johns Hopkins. I think it is a positive quality to be proud of your university and to have a sense of humor about such things. This shirt goes from jest to overconfidence only when the wearer starts believing the message.[22]

It is natural that our success will build our confidence. This is healthy. As psychologist Martin Seligman has demonstrated in numerous studies, a sense of mastery over our environment is essential for our well-being.[23] The experience of being successful in overcoming obstacles helps build our sense of mastery. Leaders need to recognize that healthy mastery is grounded in reality, but mastery becomes overconfidence when we lose sight of that reality. In the case of incoming MBA students, the delusion comes from comparing themselves selectively, but unconsciously, to a less challenging group. The MBA experience offers an opportunity to challenge that self-perception and allows the students to use their experience to create a sense of mastery rather than reinforce overconfidence.

These three overconfidence traps—not knowing what we don't know, not knowing what we used to not know, and letting successful experiences lead to overconfidence—can fortunately be minimized, provided we are willing to recognize that we may be overconfident. The simple action that can profoundly reduce overconfidence is getting in the habit of looking for evidence that we are wrong. Not only can this simple action reduce overconfidence, but, in doing so, it challenges us to break out of our current frame and actively look for disconfirming evidence.

The Hard Truth about Unconscious Bias

I am biased. So are you. We all see the world through the lens of our own experience. We all make snap judgments about people and situations on a daily basis as we navigate our lives. The cognitive path of least resistance ensures that these snap judgments and the biases that drive them will remain unconscious. They will remain the hidden operating system behind our decisions. We routinely make snap judgments based on our frame of reference, single out evidence that suggests we are right while discounting other evidence, and continually build on our inherent sense that we are correct. The hard truth is that each of us suffers from our unquestioned brilliance.

Overcoming our unquestioned brilliance requires discipline. It requires us to find routines and techniques that force us to go beyond the obvious and test our logic. The ten techniques outlined in this book help with this process and offer some structure for the hard work of breaking the cycle of the fundamental leadership trap.

Navigating Idea Translation Challenges
A Core Task of the Leader

2

> The only way to escape the corruptible effect of praise is to go on working.
> —Albert Einstein

Leaders must contend with the fundamental leadership trap in everything they do. To narrow the focus a bit, I chose to orient this book around three key organizational challenges through which every leader must be able to guide teams. These processes require active critical thinking and are particularly susceptible to being derailed by limited mindsets, confirmation bias, and overconfidence. In this chapter we take a brief detour to define the concept of idea translation, outline the three idea translation challenges that form the structure for the rest of the book, and introduce the ten techniques described in subsequent chapters.

Consider for a moment the challenge of changing behavior within an organization. First, one needs an insight, a new idea. Second, one needs the patience and skill to convert that idea into actions and behaviors. Finally, one needs to ensure that those behaviors are sustained over time. These three challenges are not just a part of organizational change; they are also the primary aims of successful leaders[1].

To be a successful leader within an organization, an executive needs to master each of these three challenges. The difficulty is that each requires quite different skill sets. In addition, each of these three challenges requires recognition on the part of the leader that the nature of the initiative itself will be modified throughout the process. During each of these challenges, the initiative is transformed in a fundamental way. The idea is translated into something new, and skilled leaders understand this and embrace it rather than fight against it.

The Importance of Idea Translation

Innovation and organizational leadership are not about knowledge transfer—they are about knowledge transformation. Traditional approaches to strategic planning and innovation often assume that the only transformation occurs during the initial idea or strategy creation. Executing and sustaining the idea is assumed to be limited to making the idea work (while changing it only at the margins, of course). This is a false assumption. It does, however, explain why many strategists behave as if the hard work is in coming up with the idea, and the actual implementation should be relatively straightforward.

The three translation challenges described in this chapter are all efforts to take a general concept and translate it into something context-specific. These challenges involve translating what anthropologist Clifford Geertz refers to as transitioning experience-far concepts into experience-near concepts.[2] Experience-far information focuses on generalizability. Leadership frameworks taught to managers would be categorized as experience-far knowledge. Experience-near information focuses on the specifics of the context, explaining what is unique and important for a given context.

For knowledge to become actionable, an actor needs to translate it from an experience-far concept to an experience-near concept. Experience-near translation challenges occur in every organization and underlie sustainable change.[3] Successful navigation of all three translation challenges, while not necessary to make knowledge actionable, may be necessary to make the actions sustainable. It is through the process of confronting the tension inherent in these challenges that the change is embedded within the routines and actions of the participants.

Idea translation is not a new concept. Translating knowledge has been at the core of discussions of epistemology for as long as scholars have debated the nature of knowledge.[4] But a translation framework is a challenge to the conventional divide between idea generation and idea execution pervasive in modern organizations. A translation framework suggests that knowledge generation cannot be separated from knowledge application. For information to transform behavior, it must become relevant within the local context. Idea translation offers one explanation for how this is done.

Barbara Czarniawska and Bernward Joerges argue that ideas do not simply move unchanged from one local setting to another but are transformed when moved into a new setting. General ideas are themselves ambiguous. They are given meaning through their connection with other ideas, through action taken on them, and through the ways in which they are translated for new settings.

Ideas That Motivate Action

The type of idea translation of interest in this book leads to insights and actions that change the organization in one way or another. Just as the movement of ideas from one context to another is not a passive process, organizational systems do not change on their own. Changes occur through the actions of individuals and, ideally, through the thoughtful actions of leaders. The academic term for the active re-creation of social patterns due to awareness of current social system limitations is *praxis*. At its core, leadership is about enabling praxis. While the term may sound academic, the concept is central to understanding how leaders can make organizations more effective.

Praxis, as defined by Richard J. Bernstein, has three key elements: (1) the recognition of existing social conditions and, more specifically, acknowledgment of how those conditions are not meeting needs; (2) the generation of a new understanding of social conditions and individuals' roles within those conditions, combined with the motivation to act; and (3) the action to rebuild roles within the existing structure as well as self-awareness of the need to change as conditions change.[5] These three elements form the basis for the translation challenges outlined in this chapter. It is the rare leader who has the skills needed to navigate each of the three translation challenges. But leaders who can do this stand out within their organizations and quickly develop a reputation for strategic thinking, creativity, and the ability to get things done.

Navigating the translation challenges is further complicated by the fact that leaders must actively contend with the fundamental leadership trap throughout each of these moments. The cognitive path of least resistance (sticking with their current mindset, discounting evidence they are wrong, believing they have the right answer) creates a strong head wind with which leaders must contend while guiding others through these challenges. Generating insight demands that leaders sincerely seek and value alternative mindsets. Transforming an idea into action requires leaders to actively look for evidence that the plan has flaws and adjust them on the fly. Sustaining new behaviors over time calls for leaders to refresh ideas and modify them over time rather than stick with initial designs.

Within each translation moment, the specific tasks of the leaders change, but the general aims do not. Leaders must act in ways that broaden mindsets, generate alternatives, and seek disconfirming evidence. The techniques outlined in this book offer some disciplined ways for leaders to structure these conversations and decision processes.

First Translation Challenge: Creating a New Mindset

The first translation challenge is the one that is most familiar to people when they think about strategic innovation. This is the moment that creates flashes of insight and generates excitement and a sense of breakthrough. The translation itself is often experienced as happening quickly. Of course, to do it well requires lots of preparation and a process that can enable a eureka moment.

To successfully guide a team through this translation challenge, leaders must overcome overconfidence and deeply held conventional mindsets, as well as a general fear of taking risks. Fortunately, leaders have many techniques available for managing this process. Scenario planning and uncertainty tracking, along with creative problem solving and innovation exercises, are excellent tools to help leaders move their teams through this first translation challenge.

It's as Simple as a Computer Model
Expertise Triggers Insight

In his book *Priests and Programmers*, J. Stephen Lansing describes the difficulty of getting government planners and Balinese priests to work together to manage the ecosystem of Bali.[6] For many years, Balinese priests had managed the flow of water through the rice terraces of Bali by setting their ceremony schedules and enabling farmers to coordinate their planting schedules around the religious calendar. With the introduction of new green-revolution rice species, the planting calendar was disrupted because the new species required differing amounts of time to grow. The government planners did not recognize the role that the priests played in managing water flows.

As the new strains of rice began to wreak havoc on the ecosystem due to water shortages and new pest infestations, Lansing set out to bridge the divide between the planners and the priests. He did this by creating a computer simulation replicating the system of water flow as managed by the water temples. This computer simulation demonstrated that it would have been virtually impossible to design a more efficient and effective way of managing water than the system that had been developed over a thousand years through water temple coordination.

Lansing effectively translated the water temple system into the language of computer simulation, which the government planners could understand and recognize.

In this example, the actual moment of translation—the creation and communication of the computer simulation—is quite short. But that eureka moment was enabled by Lansing's ability to understand both the language of religion and the language of planning. It was also enabled by the thirty years of experience that Lansing had with Bali's ecosystem. The first translation moment will be effective only with the right expertise.

Leadership Tasks in the First Translation Challenge

Primary goal	Related technique
Challenging taken-for-granted assumptions	Blind-spot centering
Finding coherent patterns in future uncertainties	Uncertainty vectoring
Testing for "Groundhog Day"-type rationalizations	Backward-forward flip

Second Translation Challenge: Converting the Insight into Action

The second translation challenge is quite different from the first one. While the first translation challenge often happens quickly, the second one takes an extended period of effort. It requires conversations with multiple stakeholders, a long-term commitment of time and resources, and leaders willing to be flexible in how the initial idea is implemented.

To make the new idea a behavioral reality, leaders must overcome entrenched routines, conflicting interests, and incompatible time cycles between the initiative and other activities within the organization. Techniques that will help leaders manage this process include structured decision processes, expertise assessments, stakeholder mapping, and influence and persuasion frameworks.

Sometimes the Best Way Forward Is to Wait
Patience as a Second Translation Strategy

Intractable stakeholder interests do not necessarily mean the translation cannot proceed. An illustrative example of this can be seen in the efforts put into signing Jackie Robinson, the first black ballplayer to play in Major League Baseball (MLB).[7] In the 1940s, Branch

Rickey, general manager of the Brooklyn Dodgers, was committed to signing the first black baseball player in the modern era.

During this period, the MLB commissioner Kenesaw Landis vigorously opposed the desegregation of the league. Landis was in a powerful position, and Rickey knew that the commissioner would do everything in his power to prevent the Dodgers from succeeding.

Today most traditional frameworks of organizational change would argue that Rickey needed to find a way to frame the change such that the commissioner would accept it or at least allow it to go forward. Rickey did not do this. He believed the commissioner could not be persuaded. Instead of trying to persuade him, Rickey waited. In November 1944, Commissioner Landis died.

It is not a coincidence that the efforts of the Brooklyn Dodgers moved quickly forward in the six months following Landis's death. Rickey recognized that it would be futile to try to persuade Landis. Rather than devoting efforts to persuading Landis, Rickey spent his time designing the initiative so that he could move rapidly once there was a new commissioner in place.

Leadership Tasks in the Second Translation Challenge

Primary goal	Related technique
Creating a team with correct expertise	TAP analysis
Preventing premature agreement on a single option	GSO decision process
Finding hidden perspectives and challenging views	Stakeholder mapping

Third Translation Challenge: Sustaining the Change

All too often a strategic initiative is viewed as successful when it has been executed successfully once. In fact, a majority of organizational change models end at the completion of the second translation moment. The leaders pat themselves on the back, check off the box saying the initiative is complete, and move on to a new task. Three years later, they will be challenged to find evidence the initiative ever took place. The change will not be sustained.

The third translation challenge is the embedding of the change into the structure and culture of the organization. It requires a translation of the initiative on a continuous basis to fit it within local routines and established structures across different parts of the organization. It also requires further attention when people shift roles within the organization.

Leaders need to fight the tendencies to prematurely declare an initiative complete, overemphasize the success of the change, and refuse to modify the initiative as the environment changes. Techniques that can assist leaders during the third translation challenge include scheduled situational assessments, active efforts to revisit the initial design of the change, and the strategic rotation of change team membership. Each of these techniques can ensure that the change initiative adapts to unique elements of different contexts. These techniques also potentially infuse the change with new energy.

The techniques for the third translation challenge described in this book confront the difficulty we often have of giving appropriate consideration to local expertise and estimating the probability of future success based on past successes. Research has demonstrated our tendency to overvalue our own knowledge and undervalue the opinion of others.[8] This even happens when we actively seek out others based on their expertise.

Design the Structure, Evolve the Culture
Sustaining a Change by Setting It Free

A privately held Italian apparel company had a great problem: It could not keep up with global demand. The company had long enjoyed a strong US market and in recent years became successful in Japan, South Korea, and parts of Southeast Asia. Now the company found unexpected new demand in South America and India too. The executive team, guided by the first CEO hired from outside the company, decided to centralize operations in Europe and reinforce a culture of quality and employee pride.

Historically, the company had let each country run its own marketing campaigns and design products to fit its culture. Although this method had contributed to company growth, the executive team was concerned that it was hurting brand quality and risked turning the company's products into high-volume, low-margin commodities. The centralization initiative was partially designed to shift to a lower-volume, higher-quality business model.

The initiative started with two work streams. The first stream began assessing the organization's current structure and identifying ways to align work and gradually move toward more centralized marketing and design. This change team had permission to design a process sensitive to individual country differences and flexible in speed of implementation but also consistent with the message that the company was committed to centralizing marketing and design decisions in Europe. The second work stream began exploring options for building a stronger corporate culture around quality and pride. This change team initially focused on internal stakeholder workshops in each country to help identify the core company culture.

The change was implemented based on data gathered in the first phase. As the change teams collected information, they also discovered individuals working in other countries with innovative ideas. In several cases, these individuals were added to the change teams as local initiative translators or full-time members temporarily relocated to Europe. The teams soon realized that the restructuring initiative could be managed as a centrally driven change initiative but that the culture change would have to be more organic and motivated by champions at the local level.[9]

The initiatives in this company had a sustained effect on the work throughout the world. The key to success was that each time the change teams visited a new country, they did not start with the assumption that they knew the plan and simply needed to replicate it. To the contrary, they entered each country with questions rather than answers. This approach allowed them to identify a plan that changed and evolved each time it was implemented.

The third translation challenge is often hardest for leaders because it requires them to give up control over the process to ensure the initiative is successfully translated to fit the needs and routines of the changing context.

Leadership Tasks in the Third Translation Challenge

Primary goal	Related technique
Identifying the challenges of local leaders	Tension tracking
Understanding the context before acting	HERE assessment
Avoiding confirmation bias	Reverse default setting

It is the rare leader who has the skills needed to navigate each one of these three translation challenges. But those are the leaders who stand out within their organizations and quickly develop a reputation for strategic thinking, creativity, and the ability to get things done.

Cycling Faster

It is tempting to view the three translation challenges as a simple linear process with a start (insight) and an end (embedding/ sustaining). The reality of leadership is not that simple. Organizations are constantly cycling through these three translations. To make things even more complex, at any given time, leaders are navigating different translation challenges on different initiatives at the same time.

Successful strategic leaders do not meticulously work through each translation moment. Rather, they are able to cycle through these translations efficiently and repeatedly to adjust to a constantly changing external environment. In their book, *Made in China*, Donald Sull and Yong Wang describe how executives at Lenovo successfully grew to dominate the Chinese PC market, not by outsmarting the executives at an equally well-positioned competing company but by more rapidly progressing through a cycle of sensing, anticipating, prioritizing, and executing in response to the rapidly changing competitive environment in the PC industry.[10]

Successful leaders don't just learn to navigate these three translation moments, move their teams beyond them, and avoid the pitfalls of the fundamental leadership trap; they also become more efficient at navigating these moments. That combination of speed and careful critical thinking is what enables an organization to maintain positive momentum. The teams do not just see opportunities missed by competitors but are also able to act on those opportunities more quickly and, if necessary, switch from those opportunities to others as the world changes.

The rest of the chapters are oriented around the ten techniques I have used while trying to help leadership teams successfully navigate one or more of these translation challenges. Each chapter focuses on a different technique. On any given project, I may use one or two of these techniques—not all of them. They form a tool kit from which I can draw when the need arises. I encourage you to view them in a similar manner.

A Note about the Techniques

The techniques outlined in the following chapters vary widely. Some are quite extensive and designed for larger groups. Others are little more than a set of systematic questions to work through. Taken together, these techniques offer a comprehensive, albeit imperfect, tool kit for the leaders who want to become more vigilant in their critical thinking and who are committed to helping their teams avoid the dysfunctional cognitive path of least resistance.

I've used each of these techniques in my facilitation work and refined them over time. But as is true with any templates for disciplined thinking, these techniques should not be approached simply as checklists or worksheets to be completed. I always remind myself at the start of any facilitation work that my primary goal is not to get through a series of exercises but to help a group work through a problem and develop some insight. The reminder helps me to embrace opportunities to improvise and modify throughout the day.

The techniques in this book are only starting points to trigger disciplined thought. You should feel free to experiment and modify the steps to fit your situation. Of course, it is also useful to walk before running and to gain some level of experience with a technique before modifying it too much.

Ten Techniques for Breaking Out of
the Fundamental Leadership Trap

Technique	Chapter
Blind-spot centering	3
Uncertainty vectoring	4
Backward-forward flip	5
TAP check	6
TAP team expertise assessment	6
GSO decision-making	7
Stakeholder mapping	8
Tension tracking	9
HERE snapshot	10
Reverse default setting	11

I chose to include the ten techniques described in the following chapters based on several criteria:

- Simplicity. Organization leaders have limited time and a dizzying array of responsibilities. I've often felt that many decision, team, and strategic thinking techniques seem designed for professional facilitators who are able to dedicate their time to learning and practicing fourteen-step frameworks with multiple templates. Recently a client showed me a decision model his organization has decided to implement. It is a well-designed model based on solid decision research. It also has thirteen steps, each with its own checklist and template. In my mind, this is not a simple technique, and for this reason it is unlikely to ever become embedded within the routine of the organization. My aim has been to make each technique as simple as possible, while still staying true to the underlying research it is derived from. I hope that short, simple steps will make it easier for busy managers to recall the technique when they need it. The TAP check, GSO decision-making process, and HERE snapshot may be the best illustrations of this principle of simplicity.

- Research. Leaders and academics are rightfully suspicious of new strategies and organizational development techniques. Not all are created equal. Because my passion is about the translation of empirical research into a form that is practical and applicable for managers, I've limited this book to techniques that have a direct relationship to research about ways to shift groups out of limiting frames, the temptation to assume knowledge, and the tendency to rationalize ideas. I limit the research references in the text but have provided them in the notes.
- Field Tests. Each of the techniques in this book has been tested with organizations of varying sizes as well as in several graduate programs in business schools. Feedback from these workshops led to modifications and, in a few cases, the rejection of techniques.
- Flexibility. I am a subscriber to the belief that no technique is a perfect fit for a given situation. Each of the ten techniques in this book can be adapted to fit the needs of the group. Once the group leader grasps the intent of a technique and the logic of the steps, I encourage experimentation. If you happen to find a modification that improves the technique, by all means, let me know!

A Humble Disclaimer

I do not claim to have invented the techniques described in this book. One thing I realized in graduate school that has stuck with me throughout my career is that social scientists are not in the business of discovering new ways humans interact. We are in the business of helping us all remember or rediscover insights about human interaction. One just needs to go back and read writings of ancient philosophers to understand that we are not treading new ground when we try to improve social interactions. We are merely translating wisdom for a new generation.

Likewise, these techniques represent some of my translations of the research of others. In some cases, such as the TAP Expertise Assessment and HERE snapshot, the techniques are ones that I developed as primary translations of research or experience. In other cases, such as stakeholder mapping or uncertainty vectoring, the techniques are modifications, inspired by my facilitation and teaching experience, of older and widely validated ones. I make every effort to acknowledge the source for these techniques, when possible.

Techniques for Generating Local Insights

First Translation Techniques: The Fun Part!

Techniques
for Generating
Local Insights

Creating insight is energizing, fun, and internally motivating for many people. For this reason, many experience the three techniques described in this section as fun. I say that as someone with years of experience facilitating groups through scenario building and blue ocean strategy workshops.[1] Scenario building and blue ocean strategy are first translation moment techniques, and both tend to energize participants. First translation techniques give people an opportunity to spend time thinking about their environment differently and to do so in a nonthreatening way. These techniques give participants license to imagine "what-if" scenarios in structured and practical ways.

- Blind-spot centering helps participants with the question, "What if our assumptions are wrong?"
- Uncertainty vectoring helps participants with the question, "What if the future plays out in a different manner than we are predicting?"
- The backward-forward flip helps participants ask, "What if we are making the same mistakes previous industry leaders made?"

Expanding Options

We often underappreciate how problem definition influences the options we generate. I suspect many of us believe that we can "out think" these externally imposed blinders and do not want to admit how easily we are manipulated.

Daniel Kahneman and Amos Tversky elegantly illustrate this "issue framing" effect in what is likely the most enduring research from their illustrious Nobel Prize–winning careers. If you offer people two options that involve equally balanced gains, they are more likely to choose the option that has less risk (is a more certain gain). For example, in one of their well-known survey questions, Kahneman and Tversky showed that a majority of people will choose a treatment option that is guaranteed to save two hundred out of six hundred people over an alternative treatment option that has a one-third chance of saving all and a two-thirds chance of saving none. When the exact same treatment options are reframed in terms of how many people will die, the majority choice switches.[2]

This research illustrates that we tend to accept additional risk in order to avoid losses and will become more conservative (risk-averse) when protecting gains. The key point here is that the choices remain the same. All that has changed is how the choices are framed. Each of us is influenced by this framing effect whenever someone tries to sell us something.

One of my favorite examples of this framing effect is a study by Liberman, Samuels, and Ross in which they found significant differences in competitive versus cooperative behavior in a prisoner's dilemma game just by titling the game either the Wall Street Game or the Community Game. The use of competitive strategy went from three in ten in the Community Game to seven in ten in the Wall Street Game. This effect far exceeded the personality effects of how competitive or collaborative the participants were perceived to be by others who knew them.[3]

I think of this study when I am working with an organization led by leaders who strongly believe that internal competition brings out the best in their managers. Leaders working within such a culture need to recognize the way it influences their choice of options. In general, a competitive mindset tends to limit options because the cooperative alternatives are often more complex. The more competitive the situation, the easier it is to simplify alternatives into win/lose, us/them choices. The situation points us toward the binary trap, which is the tendency to define a choice as a yes/no choice and limit our solution set to those two options. Moving too quickly toward the binary trap will limit creative options and often lead executives to miss the best path out of a dilemma. Unfortunately, it is also a common problem due to time pressures on making the decision. In such cases, we create our own limited mindsets.

The way you define the task impacts the options you create to solve it. If you work in a highly competitive environment, you are at risk of unnecessarily limiting your choices, and you need to be vigilant to counter this tendency. The techniques outlined in this section pull people out of the "us versus them" dynamic. These techniques create multiple views of the environment and do it without forcing participants to take sides.

All three techniques outlined in this section help break people out of conventional mindsets. One does this by directly building an alternative perspective (blind-spot centering); one does this by creating structure and clarity out of the complex and unknowable (uncertainty vectoring); and one does this by challenging people to reflect on past successes and blind spots (the backward-forward flip).

All three exercises are useful for expanding the strategic thinking processes of a leadership group. Each technique requires a different level of time commitment and addresses a different aspect of strategic thinking.

Blind-spot centering can be used to break a team out of an industry- or organization-based conventional mindset. It is a useful addition to the front end of a strategic planning meeting, to launch an innovation project, or as part of a strategic leadership training program.

Uncertainty vectoring can be used to counteract our tendencies to step into overconfidently predicting the future at the start of planning processes. It can generate a strong foundation for strategic planning and establish a language and culture of outside-in thinking within an organization.

The backward-forward flip can be used to keep a team from reinventing the wheel or to avoid falling into the same traps that hobbled previous industry leaders. It can ground a team in reality and break them out of the inevitable echo-chamber conversations based on the desire to believe "this time is different."

Blind-Spot Centering  **3**

We don't see things as they are, we see things as we are.
—Anaïs Nin

The Ubiquity of Unquestioned Mindsets

Two young fish are swimming along and happen to meet an older fish swimming the other way, who nods at them and says, "Morning, boys. How's the water?" The two young fish swim on for a bit, and then eventually one of them looks over at the other and goes, "What the hell is water?"

This little story is told at the beginning of the inspiring and quite brilliant commencement address that David Foster Wallace gave to the graduates of Kenyon College in 2005.[1] This one simple parable strikes at the core of the unquestioned mindset. Unquestioned mindsets are everywhere. All it takes to see them is an open mind and effort.

Questioning mindsets gets you to a deeper understanding of a situation. Identifying the unquestioned assumptions gives insight into the behaviors and attitudes of the actors within any given arena. Unfortunately, routines and experience conspire against us and make it hard to see the ways we frame the world. We spend much of our time operating in a somewhat automatic mode.[2] Subtle cues from our environment call up mental models from our past, and these mental models then guide what we pay attention to and how we react to our environment.

In our automatic processing mode, this use of mental models is unconscious or at least unquestioned. The advantages to using mental models are increased efficiency and an ability to learn from our experience. The disadvantage is that we may ignore those environmental cues that do not fit our mental models and selectively attend to information that does fit our mental models.[3] Not only is less information processed while we are in this automatic mode, but our selection of information is done unconsciously.

Active processing would be an alternative to this automatic use of mental models. In active processing, we pay more attention to the context and use contextual cues to create new mental models. We consciously compare the situation to different mental models we may have and actively learn through the creation of new mental connections.[4] When we seek to uncover limited mindsets, we are essentially attempting to force ourselves into an active cognitive processing mode.

For years we've recognized that questioning something that is unquestioned is a behavior that can help individuals solve intractable problems. Questioning the question and looking for ways to redefine that question form the basis for action learning techniques such as Chris Argyris's double-loop learning, Peter Senge's learning organization, as well as the numerous techniques in organizational development that have evolved from early models of action learning.[5]

Unfortunately, evidence suggests that we may not naturally recognize the need to break out of our mindsets. We naturally operate in a state of bounded awareness.[6] This may be partly because we do not even notice that we are falling into cognitive routines. Ellen Langer gives a perfect example of this in her book, *Mindfulness*. She ran a small experiment with her graduate students while teaching in the psychology department at Harvard many years ago. At the time, there was one shared copier for the floor, and there was often a line of people waiting to make copies. She instructed some graduate students to go in the room and ask to cut in line but not give any reason why they wanted to skip to the front of the line. She instructed other graduate students to go in and ask to cut in line but to give a very good reason (they were in the middle of a class exercise and ran short of copies they need to complete the exercise). She instructed a third group to ask to cut in line and give a completely random reason (something like, "Can I cut in line because I forgot my lunch?").

What she found was that few people would let the people with no excuses cut in line. A majority of people would let the people cut in line who gave reasons. In fact, there was barely any difference in the percentage allowed to cut between the individuals with the good excuse and the individuals with the bad excuse. It is as if the people in line were not actually listening to the excuses. They simply expected an excuse, and if they heard one, it fit their mental model of the situation (if I am inconvenienced, I expect the courtesy of an explanation).

How many of us realize that we have such a routine about courtesy in our mind and that we may not actually be paying attention to the logic of excuses given to us? This is an example of a routine that keeps us in our automatic mode yet is unconscious to us.

It is not just routines that may keep us locked in our mindsets. We may find ourselves so overwhelmed with surprise events in our environment that we feel threatened and fall back on our mindsets. This is called the threat rigidity response.[7] If the environment is too unfamiliar, we may reject the new information as irrelevant. If we lose our defense mechanisms, we may actually retreat to a more desperate and unrealistic set of defense mechanisms. If we experience failure, we may more vigorously defend our initial mindsets. Stress, anxiety, and high degrees of psychological arousal combine to reduce our ability to process external cues. Research in this area indicates that a moderate level of surprise in our environments can trigger a shift to active processing mode but that too much surprise may have the effect of keeping us in a defensive, automatic processing mode.

Figure 3-1 Triggering Local Insight

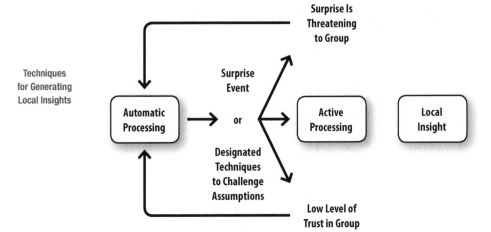

Thinking in terms of automatic and active processing redefines the challenge of creating insight into a process of switching yourself and others from automatic to active processing modes. Questioning what you see and how you frame things requires the type of situational awareness that defines active processing. Switching to active processing mode happens when you encounter something unknown or new, when you experience unexpected dissonance between what your mental model predicts and what actually happens, or when you use a process designed to consciously switch you into an active mode.[8]

Our goal as leaders is to encourage surprises and the creation of new frames but to do so in a safe, trusting environment. It is the balance of surprise and trust that maximizes the number of team members open to new ideas and actively questioning what it is they see.[9] You cannot force insight, but such a balance sets the stage for insight and hopefully increases the prevalence of eureka moments on your team (see Figure 3-1).

Blind-spot centering is such a process that can challenge assumptions but does so in a nonthreatening manner. It challenges assumptions while also potentially revealing something new and creating dissonance on the part of the participants.

Finding ways to "consider the opposite" has been found to significantly broaden our opportunity set when making decisions.[10] The blind-spot-centering exercise was derived as a translation of this decision-making research.

The Blind-Spot-Centering Exercise Steps

Step 1: Generate List of Shared Assumptions
Each person identifies three assumptions that are widely shared within the organization: one shared assumption about customers or potential customers, one shared assumption about competitors (or other relevant organizations if competition is not relevant to your organization), and one shared assumption about the organization. Combine the individual responses into a single list sorted by customer, competitor, and organization.

Facilitator Tips

I will include facilitator tips periodically throughout the book. These tips are small pointers based on my experience leading groups through these exercises.

Having people work by themselves to start things off will make step 1 go quicker and will also generate a wider range of assumptions than if the initial list is just generated by the group.

Combining the lists can also be sped up if individuals record their assumptions on sticky notes and post them on separate flip-chart pages—one page for customers, one for competitors, and one for the organization.

Step 2: Select Dominant Assumptions
Divide into three subgroups. Assign each subgroup to focus on customer, competitor, or organization assumptions. Each subgroup decides which assumption on their list is the most deeply or widely held assumption within the organization. This assumption will become the focal point for step 3.

Figure 3-2 Combined Map of Assumptions

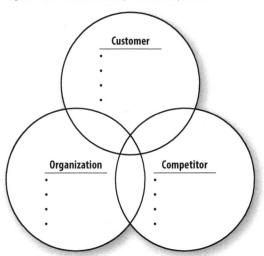

Step 3: Assumption Reversal/Blind-Spot Centering

Each subgroup is to imagine the widely held assumption selected in step 2 is incorrect. They will then generate an alternate assumption. In some cases, this may be the reverse of the original assumption. However, in some cases an assumption may be more complex than that and may not have an obvious opposing assumption. In this case, the group will need to come to an agreement around a new assumption that is incompatible with the original assumption.

Step 4: Describe the World

The subgroup answers the question: if the assumption identified in step 3 were true, what would the environment look like? List some assumptions about this imaginary world. What the group is doing is creating an internally coherent alternate reality built around the new assumption identified in step 3 How would customers be different? Suppliers? Competitors? Employees? Are there any assumptions listed in step 1 that would still hold true? If so, list these as well.

For example, take an assumption from the pharmaceutical industry as our step 2 assumption. There has been a generally shared assumption in that industry that customers will pay for

Figure 3-3 Expanding the Initial Assumption Set

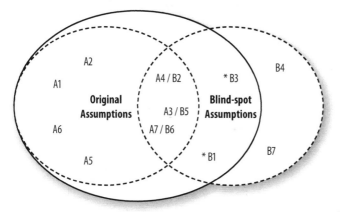

drugs with scientifically proven medical benefits. In a world where that assumption is not true, what might be true? Perhaps we are in a world of constrained resources or one in which there is a mistrust of scientific claims. Or maybe there are other more pressing concerns such as war or environmental devastation, or perhaps poor educational systems have reduced the ability of individuals to discern science from fad.

Step 5: Create a Combined Map of Assumptions

Combine the work of the three groups onto a single Venn diagram (see Figure 3-2 as an example). Make note of the overlapping assumptions. Groups should also add assumptions from the other groups to their lists if they fit and move them to the overlapping area of the Venn diagram.

Step 6: Compare Assumptions to the Original List

Compare the blind-spot centered Venn diagram to the original list of assumptions made in step 1. Highlight any assumptions that remain on both lists. These assumptions are robust and likely are strongly held by participants—so much so that participants see them still fitting within their alternate worlds. Discuss which new assumptions are realistic and ought to be used to monitor or modify the dominant mindset within the organization.

Figure 3-3 illustrates one possible output. The initial assumptions are combined with the new ones generated by the three subgroups on a single chart. The assumptions with the asterisk (*) are the new assumptions that the group identified as realistic and aligned with the initial set of assumptions. The solid line illustrates how the exercise expanded the current shared mindset to include the new assumptions. In some cases, assumptions are modified rather than being completely changed.

Using the Results of Blind-Spot Centering

The process of working through this exercise helps a group broaden its mindset and challenge conventional wisdom. The results can trigger some new insights as well. Here are some questions I often use to drive discussion after this exercise. Any one of these questions can lead to some excellent, specific actions for the group that build from the expanded mindset created through blind-spot centering.

- Are there specific stakeholders (customers, regulators, activists, suppliers) who operate out of one of the blind-spot-centered perspectives?
- After going through this exercise, do any of the widely shared assumptions identified at the beginning seem particularly at risk for not being true? What can you do to test the validity of those assumptions?
- How well would your organization do in the different worlds described in Figure 3-2?
- What is your organization doing to monitor and test shared assumptions? What could you start doing?

Value of the Blind-Spot-Centering Exercise

Limited mindsets create dysfunctions for us because, as a result of them, we may not be aware of our blind spots; we may feel pressured to support the conventional wisdom; and we may become locked into a mindset that limits our choices.

First, as I mentioned in the first chapter, we may simply not even recognize that we're operating out of a limited mindset.

We may not see other perspectives partially because we're not looking but partially because it is human nature to not question our frames of reference. Second, representing an alternate perspective, one that is not the dominant mindset in an organization or an executive team, can be politically risky. Even if it is not risky, if it is perceived as risky, it may prevent someone from sharing a different perspective. As simple as it is, the blind-spot-centering exercise addresses both of these problems.

By building new perspectives around alternatives to the most deeply held assumptions within a group, the exercise helps a group see alternate perspectives and does so in a fairly humorous way. I say "humorous" because often the blind-spot-centered perspective creates some rather absurd scenarios. By describing the extreme alternate mindsets, the group naturally sees the value in less extreme alternate mindsets. The exercise also does this in a disarming way that addresses the issue of political risk that people may feel when speaking about alternate perspectives. In the blind-spot-centering exercise, no one is required to claim ownership of the unconventional mindsets. In essence, the group gives itself permission to imagine a world in which shared assumptions do not hold true because everyone in the room recognizes that it is just part of an exercise.

The blind-spot-centering exercise also reminds us that we naturally discount anything we cannot see. This is actually the case, even when what we cannot see is important to our work. Out of curiosity, I tested this "out of sight, out of mind" tendency in my own unscientific manner over the past year.

I travel quite a bit for my work. I also live in a small town with a small airport, which means most of my travels start with a short flight on a small regional jet. Many of you may be familiar with these airplanes. One characteristic of these planes is that they have limited overhead storage space, and larger carry-on bags are "gate checked." This means they are put in the baggage hold when you enter the plane and then given back to you when you exit the plane. Depending on your arrival airport, you collect your bag one of two ways: you either exit through stairs onto the tarmac and wait for your bags next to the plane, or you exit through a gate ramp and wait for your bags to be delivered to you in the covered ramp leading to the terminal. When the passengers are waiting outside the plane, they are visible to the baggage crew; when the passengers are waiting in the ramp, they are not visible to the crew.

Once, while waiting for my bag, it occurred to me that this could be an interesting way to test the idea that what is not seen is perhaps discounted in some manner. I began timing how long it took for me to be reunited with my bag. For over a year, I tracked my fights. Sure enough, when the passengers were visible to the baggage handlers, the bags arrived more quickly. In fact, in my limited sample, the bags arrived in less than half the time. I don't claim this is in any way a well-designed, controlled experiment. Rather, it started as a way for me to pass time and to test a personal theory. I use it here less as empirical evidence and more as a vivid story to remind you about blind spots. The next time you are waiting for your bags plane-side, use that waiting time to ponder what hidden things you may be discounting in your work.[11]

Uncertainty Vectoring

4

We have two classes of forecasters: Those who don't know and those who don't know they don't know.
—John Kenneth Galbraith

I enjoy listening to a smart person prognosticate as much as the next person. Speeches and articles about the future get me thinking, and that's never a bad thing. However, I need to constantly remind myself that the author, or the person at the podium, who is telling me what is going to happen over the next five to ten years knows little more than I do about the future. Nevertheless, a good futurist is thought provoking. A thoughtful rumination on the future can be insightful for all in the room, even if the speaker is more confident in his or her predictive ability than is warranted.

We are horrible at predicting the future, but our lives require that we plan for it. Perhaps this is why we so eagerly listen to others tell us what the future will bring. We are grasping for any edge that will help us manage for the future.

In February 2014, I found myself in a room with approximately fifty experts from the oil and gas industry. We were discussing the price of oil, and everyone in the room agreed that the lowest the price of oil would go over the next twelve months was $80 per barrel. Several people in the room later confided to me that their company's capital projects were designed to be profitable anywhere above $65 per barrel. Given this, you can appreciate why most people in the room were upbeat about the prospects of their industry.

By November of 2014, fewer than twelve months later, the price of oil was less than $50 per barrel. In November, I am sure I could have found a dozen industry experts who would confidently make the case that the low price was temporary. I likely could also have found a dozen industry experts who would confidently make the case that the low price would stay with us for the foreseeable future. By the time you read this, one of these two groups of experts will have been proven right. Not only that, but looking back, it will seem obvious that they were going to be right. It is tempting for us to conclude that we would've agreed with those experts who are correct back before anyone knew they were correct.

This little trick our mind plays on us when it comes to retrospective sense making is one of the reasons we think we can predict the future. We believe we could have predicted the past. There have been several wonderful studies to illustrate this.[1] Let me explain. People are asked to estimate probabilities that something will happen, and then, after the fact, those same people are asked whether or not they thought something would happen in their earlier survey. If something does happen, participants consistently report that they gave that event much higher probability of happening in the first survey than they actually did. This hindsight bias is made worse when combined with our knowledge of how successful the actions were—the outcome bias.[2] If something did not work, we forget that we did not know it would fail before it happened.

If we are so bad at predicting the future, what are we to do? Just give up? Of course not. We still need to make plans based on our understanding of the future, but the trick is to stop trying to *predict* and start trying to *anticipate* possibilities. Planning for the future is about looking for patterns and seeing when trends end and new ones begin early enough so that we can take advantage of this.

A good example, again from the energy industry, would be the strategic actions of EOG, a US-based oil and gas company. In 2005, the time of the growing boom in shale gas production in the United States, EOG shifted its investments away from its natural-gas assets and used the proceeds to invest heavily in oil production. Shortly thereafter, the price of natural gas cratered.[3] While EOG could not predict that this would happen, its leaders anticipated the possibility that it would happen due to the sudden increase in supply that the opening up of shale deposits would have on the natural-gas market. In such competitive industries, sometimes seeing things just a few months before your competitors can be enough for you to take advantage of that insight.

Five Strategies That Can Help You Better Anticipate the Future

1. Understand trends but focus on uncertainties.
   Trends are important, but they are simply the cover charge for entering the conversation. We love talking about trends because we can see them, measure them, and project their path into the future. Of course, this means everyone else who is paying attention can also see them. Talking about trends lets others know that you understand the industry and also invites others to agree with you. Trends do not, however, give us the same level of insight about the future as do uncertainties.

   When I discuss a trend, I want to debate when a trend will end (as all eventually do) and what trend may replace it. In other words, let's talk about the uncertainty that is inherent in a trend. We can learn a lot by prioritizing uncertainties and considering how different uncertainties relate to each other. Understanding uncertainties gets you ahead of your industry; understanding trends lets you survive in your industry.

2. Know what you don't know.
   Overconfidence is pervasive. When I teach critical thinking, I routinely demonstrate that virtually every person

57

in the classroom does not accurately know what they do not know. We extrapolate what we know (or at least what we think we know) to what we don't know, and we don't even know that we are doing it. Confused by that last sentence? Good. Rereading can trigger active processing, or situational awareness, which is a first step to countering overconfidence.

When listening to futurists talk, remind yourself that they may not know what they don't know. Then ask yourself what it might be that they don't know. If you are the one speaking about the future, remind yourself that it is not about prediction; it is about possibilities. Predicting combined with overconfidence leads to single-point forecasting; single-point forecasting occurs when we try to set a single future value on some variable (for example, five-year market growth, interest rates, amount of cross-border trade). Single-point forecasts tempt us to set all our plans as if that target is guaranteed to happen. We, meaning all of us including that person at the podium, stink at single-point forecasting.

3. Listen to experts *and* outsiders.

Experts have a solid reputation for a reason. Even if they think they know more than they really know (see the previous point), they still likely know a lot. One enlightening way to start a conversation about the future of your industry is to interview six to eight industry experts and ask them to talk about key trends and uncertainties. The insight comes from seeing the pattern of ideas from multiple experts rather than listening to just one.

However, don't listen to only experts; listen to outsiders too. These may be people who are not given much legitimacy within an industry. These may be people who are discounted by industry experts. Outsiders see the world through a different lens than industry experts. Even though discounting outsiders is a well-honed industry defense mechanism tied to the confirmation bias, outsiders often know more than experts think.

I am reminded of conversations I had with executives at an automotive parts supplier in 2008. They told me that anyone who did not grow up in the auto industry could never understand it.[4] In the next breath, they told me their industry was doomed if they did not change how they perceived the world. These experts recognized they needed outsiders' points of view, yet they refused to give outsider perspectives any credibility!

4. Find patterns in complexity.

Once you dive into a conversation about uncertainties, you risk being overwhelmed by the complexity of what you find. Structured techniques can help here. Scenario building is one useful and widely used technique to sort and manage this complexity. The advantage of scenario building is that, if done well, it creates multiple plausible and different potential futures. Multiple scenarios create a counterbalance to our tendency toward overconfidence and a limited focus on the most likely future. In addition to my use of scenarios, I've refined an alternate technique, uncertainty vectoring, that can also help reveal patterns in the uncertainties.

Uncertainty vectoring maps the correlations and patterns among high-impact uncertainties, allowing a group to examine a wide array of "what-if" questions about the future. Uncertainty vectoring builds from commonly used scenario-planning processes and has much in common with them. Both work well, and both have strengths. I taught scenario planning for a number of years and designed uncertainty vectoring to address some of the common challenges I've observed with the use of scenarios. However, like any framework, uncertainty vectoring has weaknesses as well.

5. Remember you are wrong.

There is only one guarantee about your description of the future. It is wrong. This does not mean it is useless to imagine futures—quite the opposite. If we take the time to debate, discuss, and describe multiple futures, but we also recognize that none of our imagined futures will perfectly describe the true future, we become more attuned to patterns of uncertainties and more prepared to respond to emerging trends as they play out.

Uncertainty Vectoring

Uncertainty vectoring is a technique designed to counteract over-confidence in our ability to predict the future, which hobbles us in many of our planning endeavors. It has much in common with other future-focus planning tools such as scenario planning and options testing. Uncertainty vectoring offers a systematic and intuitive process to help groups consider the possible interactions among high-impact uncertainties. The focus on uncertainties rather than on trends also has the effect of pushing groups just a little outside their comfort ranges and challenging them to envision unconventional yet possible future trajectories.

The design of uncertainty vectoring takes advantage of the brain's skill at finding patterns by guiding a group through a process of building a pattern out of a set of high-impact, materially different uncertainties. This logic has much in common with analogical training, which research has shown to improve solution generation and expand options considered.[5]

This exercise is best done in a group setting, and it goes without saying that, just like any other planning exercise, it is "garbage in, garbage out." This means the people in the room ought to be the *right* people in the room. They need to have enough knowledge about the environment to keep the exercise grounded in reality. Nonexperts can certainly come up with some interesting stories using this technique, but those stories will be little more than entertaining fiction.

In this section, I outline the five steps to uncertainty vectoring and discuss several possible applications for the output of this exercise.

Step 1: Define the Destination
We need to define our focus before we can do any useful work with uncertainties. The focus needs to include the area of interest and time horizon. For our example, the area of interest is the bar industry in an American college town, and the time horizon is five years in the future.

Figure 4.1 The PEST+ Categories

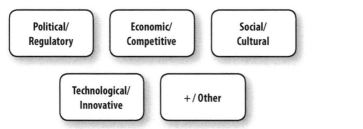

Step 2: Identify Key Uncertainties:
The PEST+ Brainstorming Structure

PEST analysis has been around for many years. The letters refer to key categories of external forces that organizations need to consider: political, economic, social, and technological. Its origins can be traced to the early work of Francis Aguilar in 1967.[6] Over the years, people have refined the categories in different ways and created numerous acronyms (STEPE, PESTLE, STEEP, STEEPER). These new formulations have added various categories such as legal, ecological, or environmental.

PEST is often referred to as PEST analysis, but this is a bit of a stretch for the word *analysis*. It is more of a memory device to help generate a diversity of forces and to ensure that you do not miss any key categories. PEST is often the first step in other forms of analysis or sense making, such as root cause analysis, scenario planning, or future state threat analysis.

I've used PEST-based techniques for many years and tried a number of different categories. I've settled on what I call the PEST+ framework. The four categories that have consistently generated the uncertainties with the highest impact are political/regulatory, economic/competitive, social/cultural, and technological/innovative. In addition, each specific application often has another category that is highly relevant to the situation. Examples could be environmental, legal, global, or even just "other." In my facilitation experience, I have found including an "other" category (see Figure 4-1) often generates some helpful additions to the other four categories that were almost missed in the initial brainstorming.

Facilitator Tip

The most common way to facilitate PEST analysis is to share the categories with the group and then have participants identify key uncertainties in each category. An alternate approach is to start by asking everyone to identify important uncertainties before introducing the PEST+ categories. I often give everyone a stack of sticky notes and tell them to write each uncertainty on a separate note. Once this is done, each person places his or her note on a flip-chart page that fits the category of the uncertainty. This approach not only helps generate lots of uncertainties quickly, it also reveals some shared group blind spots. Certain categories will be filled with sticky notes while others will be mostly empty. In addition, the "other" category will often be defined quickly, based on the notes placed there. A next step would be to challenge the group to fill in the blind spots with additional uncertainties.

Step 3: Identify the Ten Highest-Impact Uncertainties
High-impact uncertainties are those that will have the greatest impact on the end point and the path to that end point within the time horizon defined in step 1. There will be disagreement about this. After all, these are uncertainties. It is not important to rank the exact order of impact. Sorting into high-, medium-, and low-impact categories will suffice. Table 4-1 lists the top ten uncertainties in our example.

Step 4: Identify Current State on the Uncertainty Continuum
Figure 4-2 illustrates step 4 for our bar example. The line represents the range of potential outcomes for the uncertainty over the specified time horizon (five years, in our example). For each uncertainty, define the end points of the range and place an X on the point in that range that represents the current state. For example, the group completing this exercise felt it was just as likely that alcohol consumption would decrease as that it would

Table 4-1 Five-Year High-Impact Uncertainties Facing a US College-Town Bar

U1	Change in alcohol consumption patterns
U2	Disposable income for under-thirty age group
U3	Area population growth
U4	Change in beer consumption
U5	Ability to find staff
U6	Increase in professionals/noncollege students
U7	Trends for home entertaining
U8	Number of competing bars
U9	Change in state allocation of liquor licenses
U10	Growth in out-of-town visitors

Figure 4-2 Current State of High-Impact Uncertainties

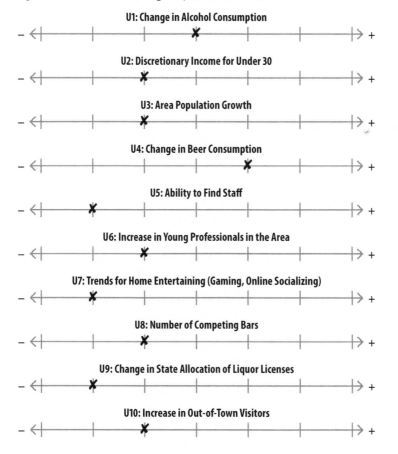

Figure 4-3 Uncertainty Vectoring Chart

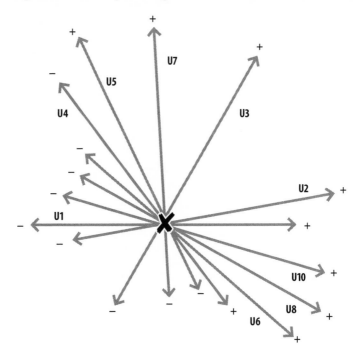

increase over the next five years, so that X is placed in the center slash mark on the arrow. For the increase in discretionary income uncertainty, the group felt there was more upside movement likely over the next five years, so they placed the current state X farther to the left on the line. Do this for each of the ten uncertainties.

Step 5: Create the Uncertainty Vector Chart

The uncertainty vector chart is the primary output of the uncertainty vectoring exercise. It creates a visualization of uncertainty relationships. The resulting chart gives a group a tool for organizing and discussing a complex mix of high-impact uncertainties. The generation of the chart creates a way to structure a conversation about the important but unknown elements of the industry.

Figure 4-3 shows what a completed uncertainty vector chart looks like. We start with a blank white space. A flip chart will work, although I have found a whiteboard or two combined with flip charts often work better. In the center of the space place an X.

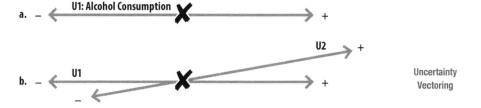

Figure 4-4 Marking the Vectors

a. — U1: Alcohol Consumption + ✖

U2 +

b. — U1 ✖ +
   —

Pick one of the ten high-impact uncertainties in which the current state X, created in step 4, is close to the center of the uncertainty line. Set this line as your horizontal anchor and mark the end points to indicate directionality as shown in Figure 4-4a.

Measure the length of the line. It is important that you draw each subsequent uncertainty line to the same length as this first line. This is why I included the slash marks in Figure 4-2.

Next, from the remaining nine uncertainties, choose a second high-impact uncertainty that is the most highly correlated with the first selected uncertainty. Add this uncertainty to your map as shown in Figure 4-4b. Notice the current state X created in step 4 is lined up with the X in the center of the uncertainty vector map. Pay attention to the directionality of the correlation with the first uncertainty and align your lines accordingly (make certain the +/- poles reflect the nature of the relationship with the other uncertainties).

Continue this process with the third uncertainty. Each time you add a new uncertainty to the map, discuss correlations with your group. It is in this process of deciding the order of adding the uncertainties and the strength and directionality of relationships among the uncertainties that your group begins to develop a deeper understanding of how these uncertainties interact with each other.

Continue this process until you have added all ten uncertainties to your map. It is likely that there will be some disagreement within your group about how uncertainties relate to each other. That is to be expected. After all, you are talking about uncertainties in future states; by definition, these positions are difficult to measure and predict. Work to find some compromise, but also make note of those uncertainties that are particularly difficult to place on the map. Your team may want to devote some additional time to think about these uncertainties or to discuss what additional data you could collect to generate a better understanding of them.

Facilitator Tips

It is sometimes tempting to create this map by starting with two uncertainties that are the least correlated with each other rather than with two uncertainties that are highly correlated with each other. In this case, one is placed on the horizontal, and one is placed on the vertical axis. This approach can work and is, in fact, the basis for the most widely used scenario building techniques. I have found that if you start with two highly uncorrelated uncertainties, you often find yourself in a bind when it comes to drawing the final two or three uncertainty lines. By building from most correlated to least correlated, we use an incremental process, which is akin to building a story. The most uncorrelated uncertainty reveals itself naturally if we focus the conversation (set our frame) on similarity.

In addition, in many cases the two least correlated uncertainties still have some level of correlation. In these cases, you will not have any line that is vertical and perfectly perpendicular to your starting line. In such cases, the uncertainty vector map may better reflect reality than a scenario building technique that creates a scenario space by setting one uncertainty on the horizontal and one uncertainty on the vertical.

It is important that all your lines be the same length. Use a measuring stick or a piece of string to measure the length of the first line before you draw the other lines. It is also important to line up your X's, so pay attention to the location of the current state X on each uncertainty line.

Try not to get bogged down in deep discussions about strength of correlations. The first time you draw your uncertainty vector map, it will likely be messy, and once or twice you will find the need to cross out and redraw a line. Assume that you will need to redraw a final version after you have discussed all ten uncertainties.

If you have an uncertainty that seems to have no correlation whatsoever to any of the other nine uncertainties, decide if there is a

placement of this uncertainty that leads to a more interesting strategic story of the future and place the line there. I find it useful to note
these lines as outliers, and I do not use them as the primary focal
point for subsequent strategic work using the uncertainty vector
chart.

Using the Uncertainty Vector Chart

Once you've created the uncertainty vector chart, you can use it
as a framework for structuring a number of different strategic
conversations.

"What-if" Analysis

The uncertainty vector chart adds some discipline to those frequent "what-if" conversations. The chart visually shows what may
happen to other key uncertainties if any given uncertainty moves
in a particular direction. Figure 4-5 gives an example of this for
our college bar application. The question is what will happen if
there is a dramatic decrease in discretionary income among those
under thirty. By drawing lines to the other vectors, we start to see
a story emerge explaining how the other uncertainties may play
out in such a situation. In this case, we would expect a reduction in
alcohol and beer consumption as well as in competition. It would
also be easier to find staff partially because there would be fewer
competing bars in town and partially because there would be more
underemployed young adults. However, the uncertainty vector
chart suggests that there may be opportunity in this future. It is
an open question as to whether or not there is an overall increase
in in-home entertainment depending on what happens with the
over-thirty demographic group. It is conceivable that there is an
opportunity to reorient bar business toward an older clientele who
had not frequented bars in the past due to the preponderance of
younger patrons.

Using the same uncertainty vector chart, we could build a story
based on any of the ten uncertainties. For example, we could use
this uncertainty vector chart to describe the future in which there
is a move away from in-home entertaining options. This could be

Figure 4-5 "What-If" Analysis

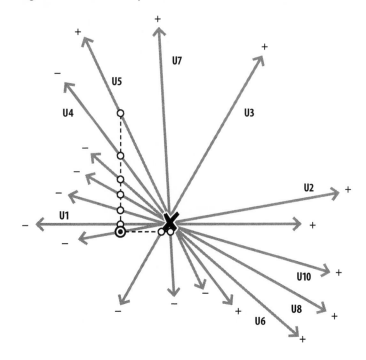

an interesting exercise because so much has been written about the growth of online entertainment that we may not have spent much time thinking about a situation in which this trend reverses and people seek out social interaction. In this case, we see a world where there are far more patrons and increased alcohol consumption. Yet there are also more competing bars, and it is a more challenging environment for recruiting good staff. In fact, it may be even more difficult to recruit good staff because there may have been an overall outflow of people from the area as adults move away from a small college town in order to experience the more dynamic social life of a larger city.

After doing this exercise with several uncertainties, the group will start to recognize which uncertainties seem to be the most strategically relevant to their job. The group also starts to recognize potential leverage points—uncertainties they might be able to influence to drive toward a future that is advantageous for their organization. Often this exercise reveals some counterintuitive insights. For example, perhaps your bar is actually more successful in an environment characterized by less competition and lower overall demand because ease of staff recruitment leads to more loyal staff and a better ability to distinguish your bar from competitors.

Build Scenarios

As I stated at the beginning of the chapter, the uncertainty vectoring technique is a close cousin of scenario building techniques. The difference is that the focus remains on the uncertainties, and the step of converting the uncertainties into scenarios is removed. In the next section, I further discuss the trade-offs between uncertainty vectoring and scenario building. However, it is still possible to build scenarios from your uncertainty vector chart. To do so, simply divide your map into four quadrants and use those quadrants to describe four different scenarios. Alternatively, you could build scenarios from multiple "what-if" situations. The scenarios do not need to be forced into the four quadrants but could be pulled from any combination of uncertainties that are on your map. It is this flexibility in application that led me to develop the uncertainty vector chart in the first place.

Identifying Predictive Blind Spots

The uncertainty vector chart visually reveals future directions that your group views as outside the realm of possibility. Going back to our bar example, the shaded area in Figure 4-6 indicates the realm of futures that the group views as likely or at least feasible. The question marks indicate a potential blind spot in their mindsets. The group can take these blind spots and examine them through a blind-spot-centering exercise. This is an excellent way to prevent the uncertainty vector chart from becoming yet another piece of data that is used to feed our overconfidence and potentially lead us further into confirmation bias.

Monitor Uncertainties

At a minimum, your team should use this exercise as an opportunity to discuss how you are tracking uncertainties. Since most organizations dedicate a majority of their planning resources to tracking trends, it is likely that your team does not have a plan

Figure 4-6 Visualizing Blind Spots

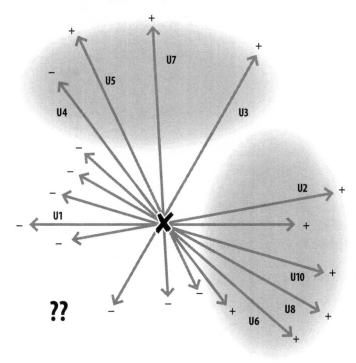

in place for tracking the ten high-impact uncertainties. For each uncertainty, consider what the early warning signs are that the uncertainty is moving in a certain direction, what data resources are available to track this uncertainty, how often your team should review this data, and what you would consider to be the tipping point for this uncertainty such that your team can now confidently view it as a predictable trend.[7]

The Trade-offs between Uncertainty Vectoring and Scenario Planning

As I noted, I have extensive experience running scenario building workshops, and it is this experience combined with my previous work on issue framing that led to my shift toward a focus on uncertainties. I absolutely believe that scenario building has great value and is the appropriate technique to apply in many situations. I am most familiar with the scenario building technique described by Paul Schoemaker,[8] since this is the foundation of most of my scenario building work. However, I've had the opportunity to experiment with other similar approaches during my time teaching a graduate class in scenario planning.[9] My contrast of uncertainty vectoring and scenario planning focuses primarily on the two scenario building techniques outlined by Schoemaker and Van der Heijden.

Benefits of Uncertainty Vectoring over Scenario Planning
- Time commitment: Many books on scenario planning suggest that it takes weeks and a commitment of resources to create solid scenarios. The largest time sink in the process is the shift from uncertainties to scenarios. This is when complexity is initially removed (narrowed to two or three uncertainties) and then built back in (detailed stories are crafted around the scaffolding of the two to three selected uncertainties). Uncertainty vectoring tries to capture some of the insight gained from building scenarios through the process of debating the correlations among uncertainties. By sticking with uncertainties, this can be done in less time, and group members tend to not get quite as lost in the process since they are still looking at their original list of uncertainties.
- Ease of revision: It is often helpful to revisit and revise uncertainty vector charts or scenarios every six months or so as the future unfolds. If there are fundamental shifts in uncertainties during that time, it can be difficult to get previously built scenarios to still fit the situation. With an uncertainty vector chart, it is simply a case of shifting a few of the vectors and seeing how it changes the story. The rest of the chart remains and does not need to be rebuilt.
- Reduced risk of either/or thinking: Good scenario planners vigilantly work to keep people from focusing too much on the top two uncertainties that anchor the scenarios. However, the nature of building futures off a limited set of realistic stories adds to the risk that we start to view the future as becoming either scenario A or

scenario B. Keeping numerous uncertainties front and center in the final end product of the process can help avoid this risk.

- Closer link to environmental monitoring: It is more helpful and practical to monitor uncertainties than it is to monitor scenarios. As uncertainties shift, the uncertainty vector chart hints how that shift may cascade across other uncertainties. This dynamic is masked within the scenario building process.

- Maintains the complexity of uncertainty interactions: This is a trade-off. The power of the scenarios is in their ease of communication and their ability to take the complexity of an uncertain future and transform it into something more manageable and understandable. However, the complexity never goes away. The focus on uncertainties in the end product keeps that complexity visible and challenges leaders to remember that none of us can predict the future.

Benefits of Scenario Planning over Uncertainty Vectoring

- Harnessing the power of stories: Stories capture attention. A well-designed set of scenarios can force participants to acknowledge the limits to their ability to predict the future better than almost any other persuasive device. Scenarios communicate industry uncertainty extremely well. They make the daunting task of planning for an uncertain future seem more doable. To put it in the idea translation context of this book, well-developed scenarios translate an experience-far concept (industry uncertainty) into an experience-near concept (rich, realistic stories of the future).

- Enables future-focused alignment: The very aspect of scenario planning that makes it time-consuming as a process (the meticulous building of well-structured scenarios) also makes it a valuable tool for creating strategic alignment throughout a global enterprise without slipping into tunnel vision. Many companies have used scenarios as a way to challenge managers at all levels to consider multiple futures when they set their plans.

Companies have also developed sets of linked scenarios to align global strategies with local strategies.

- Creates structure for conversations with stakeholders: Building scenarios is a useful way to engage outside stakeholders in strategic conversations. They also offer a valuable way to begin conversations about customers' strategic needs. The engaging nature of the stories makes this possible.

- Is widely used with well-developed follow-on tools: The fact that scenario planning has been around for over forty years means that many facilitators, consultants, and planners are familiar with it as a technique. This also means that many people have already developed excellent ways to apply scenarios.

The bottom line is that both uncertainty vectoring and scenario building are valuable techniques for countering limited mindsets and overconfidence when planning for the future. I see value in focusing attention on the uncertainties rather than on the building of scenarios; however, either process can help your team think more broadly about strategic choices, and both techniques are far better than single-point forecasting.

Predictions of the future anchor our understanding of the present. The predictions drive strategies and form the basis for conventional wisdom. They are also the raw material of limited mindsets. Uncertainty vectoring can broaden the conversation and trigger local insights based on unconventional futures.

The Backward-Forward Flip   5

Whoever wishes to foresee the future must consult the past.
—Machiavelli

Past Is Future

You've likely heard the phrase "best thing since sliced bread."
In point of fact, sliced bread was a significant innovation in the
baking industry when it was introduced in 1928. It was immediately embraced by consumers and led to significant increases
in bread consumption. It also contributed to new demand for all
those yummy jams we spread on bread.

Not surprisingly, sliced bread was not universally embraced by
bakeries. Some did not want to spend the money for the bread-
slicing machines. Some were convinced it was a fad. Many were
convinced that what they perceived as a tiny improvement in convenience for the consumer was more than offset by the loss of

quality in the bread: slicing bread destroys the protective crust that keeps the loaf fresh. Demand, however, quickly pushed aside bakers' resistance. By 1930, Wonder Bread started selling sliced bread nationally, and the sandwich was never the same.[1]

The bakers' initial suspicion is what interests me in this story. Every innovation has naysayers. Every new idea will be criticized. This is where it gets tricky. Most of the time, the naysayers are right. It is so tempting to say innovators must ignore the critics. However, there is wisdom in listening and wisdom in fighting the urge to discount criticism as uninformed.

The line between industry-transforming innovation and self-deluded rationalization (powered by the confirmation bias) is a subtle one. This line will likely be missed by the idea champion without some forced, disciplined thinking. I am reminded of Carmen Reinhart and Kenneth Rogoff's book, *This Time Is Different: Eight Centuries of Financial Folly*. Each financial innovation and subsequent financial crisis is preceded by well-argued expert opinions explaining why "this time is different" and why the old rules do not apply.[2]

We desperately want to believe that our idea is brilliant, not folly. Our bias will be toward discounting warnings that the innovation is folly. Our temptation is to attack the critic as afraid of change or limited in perspective. Not only do we want to be the one who discovers the sliced bread of our industry, we also want to make sure we are not the bakers who discount it.

The past can help you learn to distinguish between the great innovation and the deluded idea. I developed the backward-forward flip exercise as a way to consider past industry innovations as well as past resistance to those innovations in order to more creatively and critically examine today's potential industry transformations. Think of this as a quick way to stress-test your ideas before learning the hard way that your brilliance is actually folly.

Walmart, Google, Apple…

Successes are fun to study but oh so hard to replicate. At any point in time, there is a company that becomes the totem for business success. Through no fault of their own, these companies become the bane of existence for the hapless executives who are forced to sit through speech after speech after executive training after conference workshop extolling the virtues of this company. Ten years ago it was Walmart[3]; five years ago it was Google, and today it is Apple. If you are a speaker, professor, or trainer reading this and currently use one of these companies as an example, I suggest you carefully observe your audience as you tell the story. You may notice an unusually large number of people with glazed eyes and bored expressions. Don't worry; it's not you. It's your tired example. These are exemplary companies, but we are sick of hearing people tell us how we can become more like them. Rather than focusing on the successful company of the day, consider examining lesser-known successes and failures that resonate more with the given audience.

Every industry has its own sliced bread. A focus on these missed opportunities and missed signs by industry experts can be quite informative as either a complement to, or a replacement for, that new story about Apple you're just dying to tell.

Backward-Forward Flip Steps

The confirmation bias tells us that we look for evidence that we are correct. The backward-forward flip is a simple exercise designed to get a group to simultaneously consider being wrong and right. This exercise is a translation of research that has shown it is possible to counteract the hindsight bias—a form of the confirmation bias in which we believe we could have predicted a particular outcome beforehand by confronting and examining contrary evidence and explicitly taking an outsider's perspective.[4]

The group starts by dissecting the arguments for and against the success of some transformative moment from their industry's past. This process is then replicated on a current debate occurring within their industry. There is no need to overcomplicate this exercise. I have seen this exercise lead to fundamentally exciting insights about the current state of an innovation. I've also seen this exercise trigger little more than a fun conversation with little insight. It takes little time, and the upside potential for the conversation makes that time investment worthwhile. One word of caution though: this exercise works best when working with people who have extensive industry experience.

Step 1: Identify a Surprise Event from the Industry Past

Identify two to three industry surprises defined as events, shifts, or innovations that were not predicted, or even expected at all, by conventional industry wisdom. It is often difficult to generate this list in a short amount of time. For this reason, it helps to ask everyone to come to a meeting having already thought of one industry surprise event or to generate this list prior to the meeting in some other way.

For our example, we will use the rapid emergence of online book buying in the US retail book business. Given how ubiquitous online book purchases are now, it is hard to recall that there was initially significant skepticism that people would be willing to purchase their books online. The upheaval in the US retail book business that immediately preceded the emergence of Amazon was driven by the immense success of large destination bookstores such as Barnes & Noble and Borders Books. In some ways, the transformation of the industry driven by the large book retailers paved the way for Amazon by creating the expectation that any book should be available for purchase at any retailer. However, the primary transformation was in the opposite direction of the online book-buying experience.

Barnes & Noble focused on creating a welcoming community space, thus making the book-buying experience more of a social experience as well as an experience of discovery. A consumer could walk into a Barnes & Noble store and find an inviting space that encouraged them to stay, browse, and read. The immense success of this model pushed the industry conventional wisdom toward the perception that consumers wanted the physical experience of touching and enjoying a book before purchasing it. Given this setting, perhaps it's not surprising that the rapid success of Amazon caught many in the retail book industry off guard.

Step 2: Justifications for Conventional Wisdom—Past

List all the reasons industry experts gave at the time to explain why people would not buy books online:

- People want to touch/feel books before buying them.
- Readers enjoy discovering new books, and they cannot do that in an online bookstore. They want to browse.
- The industry is no longer fragmented. The big retailers now have the scale needed to match discounts.
- Only a small percentage of retail customers special order books, so there is no evidence that lack of selection is even an issue anymore now that Barnes & Noble increased in-store selection.
- The economics do not make sense for a new entrant. Margins are tightly controlled in traditional bookstores, and publisher relationships matter.
- If anyone could make online book buying work, it would be an industry player with a large network of physical stores and established industry relationships.

Step 3: Why Conventional Wisdom Was Wrong—Past

List all the reasons industry experts were wrong in their assessment. What had conventional wisdom missed? What the conventional wisdom in the retail book-buying industry got wrong:

- The ISBN number book system had made it possible to find and track books from distributors and publishers all over the world.
- Books were the ideal size for efficient shipping and storage, particularly if they could be stored with no consideration paid to retail display. Many books could even take advantage of media mail rates.
- Online book reviews and site links could replace the fun of browsing.
- Book purchasing and the enjoyment of browsing a bookstore were two separate consumer services.
- Shopping online provided a new form of entertainment that competed with the enjoyment of bookstore browsing.

Step 4: Identify a Current Potential Industry Shift

Identify a high-impact industry shift that a majority of industry experts currently do not expect to occur. This should be a shift that realistically could happen, and if it did happen, it would have a significant effect on how business operates in the industry.

Sticking with our example of the retail book-selling industry, we will consider the possibility of a significant swing back toward traditional paper books and away from digital books.

Step 5: Why This Shift Will Not Occur

Step 5 mirrors step 2 except that we are now considering the question as it relates to the current potential industry shift.

List the reasons most industry experts believe this shift will not occur, or at least why people will not shift back to traditional paper books in large numbers:

- Tablets are ubiquitous.
- People have gotten used to consuming text in digital form.
- Quality of screen has improved to the point it is similar to reading a paper book.
- Economies of e-book production will increasingly make e-books cheaper than paper books.
- Paper book sales are flat while e-book sales are experiencing rapid growth.

Step 6: Why This Shift Will Occur

List the changes in the world that would enable and potentially trigger the industry shift to occur. This list may include a wide range of changes in the environment. These could include changing preferences, triggering events, or hidden and/or unknown customer preferences.

Why people will shift back toward paper books:

- Power reader (those who purchase more than fifteen books per year) preferences shift back toward paper books. This possibly is driven by an innovative and effective marketing campaign by a national book retailer.
- Connected nature of tablets is increasingly viewed as a distraction rather than a feature for readers. Readers desire the ability to "tune out," which paper books provide.
- The growing trend toward authentic consumerism makes paper books stylish and hip.

- More efficient printing and reduced marketing expenses lower prices for paper books.
- Maker of a popular e-reader platform goes out of business or stops production of the product.
- Schools and libraries reduce their budgets for e-books.

Step 7: Rank the Probability of Items Identified in Step 6

Sort the list created in step 6 from most to least likely to occur. Starting with the most likely to occur and moving to the least likely item on the list, discuss the most likely scenario that could lead to this industry shift. What are the early indicators that the industry is moving in this direction? What organizations and individuals stand to benefit if this happens? What are those people or organizations doing right now to nudge the industry in this direction? What should your organization do to prepare for the possibility that this shift could occur?

The biggest barrier to learning from our past is our mindset that looking back will slow us down. All too often we do not recognize that reflecting on past actions, either successes or failures, is part of the work of innovation. Reflection is an action. This is an important framing because we have a bias toward action. One example of the action bias is that elite soccer goalkeepers have a bias toward moving during penalty kicks even when their success can be improved by standing still.[5] The backward-forward flip technique helps make reflection action for your team.

The backward-forward flip challenges potentially limiting conventional mindsets by looking back at the past in much the same way that uncertainty vectoring does this by looking forward toward the future. The exercise does not take long. It would be an hour well spent for your team if it helps them distinguish brilliance from folly.

Finding Your Personal Source for New Mindsets

Chapters 3 through 5 are all about generating new insights. Yet we can still be left with a challenge: where do we get our inspiration for seeing things differently?

If you examine lists of successful self-help or even management books, you will notice that many of them are based on a premise of translating an idea from one context to another... sports to work life, biology to decision-making, kindergarten to life, parenting to management, movies to parenting, religion to virtually everything. One key to being a successful translator in your work is to find something you know and are passionate about that is outside your work life and use that to create translations that are meaningful to you. (You can take this as a suggestion to cultivate and maintain interests outside your work.) When your connections bring something new into your work setting, you begin to see how idea translation can have a powerful impact.

One barrier that prevents many professionals from questioning their brilliance and looking for inspiration outside their professional field is self-inflicted professional delusion. Specifically, we accept as a given that our profession trained us to be better thinkers than practitioners in other professions, and thus we discount frameworks from outside our field. This is a dangerous mindset, because if we do not question it, it will cause us to discount the value of seeking inspiration from outside our field.

The field that most visibly illustrates this type of unquestioned brilliance is economics. Economists are less likely than those in other social science fields to cite research or theory from outside their field in publications or to believe that interdisciplinary research is of greater value than research within a single discipline.[6] It is easy to pick on the field of economics since it is a visible, influential field. However, any field of intellectual inquiry or professional training must struggle with this dilemma. Before we seek inspiration outside our fields, we must first accept that alternate approaches to thinking and alternate theories of social action may be as valuable as the one that our professional training has caused us to view as primary.

Theater to facilitation is a translation that has profoundly helped me. I do not have vast experience in theater. Like many, I acted in high school and a bit in college. However, I do have the pleasure of being married to a wonderfully gifted actor who also teaches theater at the university level. Through conversations with her, as well as my periodic forays back into acting during my adult life, I've learned from my experience as an actor or audience member and translated those experiences into my facilitation techniques. For example, with a skilled actor, you can truly sense that they are present in the moment. They are not merely repeating words and movements that they have done day in and day out. They are responding to the actors—and, in some cases, the audience—in a focused, moment-to-moment manner. Each performance can be subtly different because each night the other actors will respond in a slightly different way. The plot remains the same, but the emotions may shift. As an audience member, this may be the key difference that I observe between professional theater and community or student theater productions.

I take the importance of using attentive, active processing to connect with audiences very seriously in my work. Being in the moment means that every keynote is different; every class is unique. Borrowing theater techniques, however amateur I may be as an actor, has helped me learn how to translate those techniques to be effective in my work life. Each context has its own challenge and requires a different translation. When I teach executive classes or give a keynote speech, it is easy to be in an active processing mode because all attention is focused on me. However, it is also hard to avoid automatic processing because, in many cases, I have delivered that same content hundreds of times to thousands of people. This is the part of my work that is perhaps the most like acting. A good teacher is also a good entertainer...much as this truth may pain many brilliant people I know who seem irritated that they should be expected to entertain while they try to educate.

It is when I am in the role of facilitator that translating from theater is most challenging but also most valuable. It is easy to focus on the situation as a facilitator because your entire job is to move a group in a certain direction. The content of conversation is owned by the group, and you cannot lead a group without listening and focusing. It is difficult to be constantly attentive because you do not control the plot, and ceding time to others can be even more frustrating. This means a skilled facilitator needs to be able to let others be heard, keep things moving forward, monitor emotion and energy levels in the room, politely rein in certain people, and nudge others to contribute more. As a facilitator, you open yourself to unexpected reactions and new revelations in a way that skilled actors do.

The translation of theater exercises to facilitation work is one of my translations. What could be yours? Perhaps you are a runner, a rock climber, an avid soccer fan, a cook, or a lover of mystery novels. Find that passion and own it in your work as well. If you are reading this right now and thinking to yourself, "I used to have those interests, but right now I only have time for my work," then take this as a challenge to reclaim a passion outside your work life. In studies of successful leaders in business and elsewhere, a common theme is leaders usually have interests outside their work.

The techniques outlined in this section provide some processes to encourage new mindsets, but in the end, the content of the new mindsets will come from the diversity of experiences represented by the participants in the activity.

Techniques for Transforming Insights into Actions

Second translation techniques are all about the people. The tough work of translating an insight into an action requires coordination and mobilization of others; whereas, unquestioned brilliance leads to systematic discounting of others because other people have an irritating habit of disagreeing or asking pesky questions. It is easier to simply tune them out or limit your attention to the project plan.

This is the moment when strategic plans start to assume the dangerous mantle of unquestioned brilliance as well. Leaders grow hesitant to change the plan. The plan takes on an almost religious significance...a token of power. It is as if the plan had been created by higher-order beings with greater wisdom, so it must be followed as if it came directly from the hand of God. To suggest changes to the plan would be blasphemy and may even risk banishment. Though this may be a humorous overstatement, changing any plan does require additional effort. It also carries additional risk. Few people are fired for merely following a plan.

The fundamental leadership trap combination of limited mindsets, confirmation bias, and overconfidence combines with the pressure to show progress and thus drives leaders to focus so much on managing the tasks that they lose sight of the need to understand the people. When pressured to meet a deadline, project-management checklists create the illusion of progress. Unfortunately, those checklists often tell you nothing about the quality or appropriateness of the tasks.

The techniques I outline in this section focus on the people. First, you must find the right people for the task—those with the task knowledge needed to prevent limited mindsets. Second, you must make decisions with others in a manner that defends against the natural pressure to downplay options and limit real alternatives. Third, you must seek stakeholders who will challenge the ideas and avoid making decisions on preconceived notions about what stakeholders think.

The techniques outlined in chapters 3 through 5 help a leader think differently and potentially see new opportunities, and they are consistent with developing the strategic thinking competencies of a team.[1] Now the techniques outlined in the next three chapters help a leader mobilize others to act and set an initiative in motion. These techniques are aligned with the goal of developing change-leadership skills. Being skilled at strategic thinking without also being skilled at leading change puts a leader in that large category of organizational managers who are described as "a brilliant person, great ideas...never seems to be able to get things done." Being skilled at leading change without also being skilled at strategic thinking puts a manager in that category of people who "are great at getting things done but never seem to be able to improvise when the situation changes."

As with the techniques outlined in Part II, I assume that all three techniques outlined in these next chapters may not be valuable for you. I encourage you to focus on the one that is for your own development and use the others as a guide for how you can develop the leadership capacity of your team. I have not found many managers who are equally skilled at finding the right people, getting those people to consistently make high-quality decisions, and managing external stakeholders. However, those who are able to do all three of these tasks well rarely find themselves short of professional opportunities.

TAP Analysis 6

There's no such thing as knowledge management; there are only knowledgeable people. Information only becomes knowledge in the hands of someone who knows what to do with it.
—Peter Drucker

The Right People for the Right Task

How often do you think about the expertise of your teams? The odds are not often enough. At least, that is the finding of my research on expertise in teams. A majority of team leaders report considering team member ability when forming teams, but less than 30 percent report they systematically consider team member ability each time they assign new tasks to the team, and less than 15 percent report they consider team member ability when the team is confronted by an unexpected challenge.

In addition, in a study of help-seeking behavior in cross-functional teams, members sought help from the team expert only 17 percent of the time when encountering a problem within that expert's domain of expertise.[1] In general, we do not consider expertise enough, and when facing new challenges, we certainly do not act often enough on our knowledge of who has expertise.

Choosing the wrong people to implement a new idea is a common source of limited mindsets. The first translation techniques outlined in the previous section deal with the challenge of "seeing" a new opportunity or a new way of seeing things. Now we step back for a moment to consider the actual people we invite to participate in the process. TAP analysis is a technique designed to help a leader identify the right people for the right task. In this chapter, I describe two uses for TAP analysis: identifying the right people for the right task, and taking an expertise snapshot to assess potential gaps and strengths of a continuing team.

TAP analysis stands for task ability person analysis. TAP analysis is a direct translation of some fairly robust social science research on the use of team expertise to address a widespread team leadership challenge.[2] In my work as a coach and facilitator of executive teams, I continually meet leaders confronting similar team expertise challenges. They ask: How do I select the right people for specific teams and task forces? How can I make sure that my continuing team is developing their skill set in order to succeed?

My attempts to help answer these questions formed the genesis of TAP analysis, while two insights from academic writing and research influenced my design of TAP analysis: first, my own work attempted to create a context-specific way of measuring team expertise[3]; second, a conceptual article suggested refocusing the unit of analysis when considering team expertise away from the team and away from the individual and to a unit consisting of a combination of task, expertise, and person (a form of reframing).[4]

Knowing What Others Know: The Research

Research on expertise recognition in decision-making groups suggests that work groups perform better when their members know who is good at what. The transactive memory framework provides an explanation for these findings. Wegner introduced the concept of transactive memory systems as a way to understand how couples coordinate to solve information problems.[5] Wegner defined the transactive memory system as a combination of the knowledge possessed by each individual and a collective awareness of who knows what. He argued that this system provides individuals with access to a level of knowledge that no one member could hope to remember.

Subsequent research has extended the concept of transactive memory to help understand how to more effectively share knowledge within teams. In research that I conducted in mature, semiautonomous decision-making groups, I found evidence that a group's transactive memory system—measured as a combination of knowledge stock, knowledge specialization, transactive memory consensus, and transactive memory accuracy—is positively related to the group's goal performance as well as external and internal group evaluations.[6]

This research empirically demonstrated that building a highly functioning expert group involves more than simply assembling a group of individuals with a wide range of specialized knowledge. Although this knowledge base may establish a strong foundation for a successful group, actual group performance depends upon how well the individual members are able to tap into the assembled knowledge base and how well the individual members are able to reconfigure this knowledge base in new situations. The techniques I used to measure and evaluate group transactive memory formed the basis for the TAP Team Expertise Assessment described later in this chapter.

Framing around Tasks, Not Teams

When we consider team leadership, we often use the team as our primary point of reference. TAP analysis requires a subtle reframing to consider the task as the appropriate point of reference. Each individual team deals with multiple tasks that change over time. An expertise-based framework for team leadership requires a team leader to frequently reevaluate team process because, as tasks change, expertise demands change as well.

Brandon and Hollingshead offer an excellent framework for linking this task-oriented framing with team member expertise.[7] They proposed the task-expertise-person (TEP) unit as the basic construct for transactive memory. A full TEP unit would include knowledge about the task, expertise requirements for the task, and persons having expertise. Any missing information in a given TEP unit would need to be obtained in order for that unit to fully contribute to transactive memory in a group. Errors or missing information in any one of the three components can contribute to reduced efficacy in a group. They propose that transactive memory development involves the building of complete TEP units by group members. Accuracy, sharedness, and validation (degree of participation in the transactive memory system by group members) are the dimensions along which transactive memory systems differ. Finally, they propose that high levels of these three dimensions are characteristic of effective and well-developed transactive memory systems.

The TEP framing offers an approach that connects the cognitive and behavioral components of group coordination.[8] Accuracy and sharedness are cognitive, while validation has a behavioral component to it. All three components are developed through group interaction on multiple tasks. This task-based framing of group leadership also addresses the local versus general knowledge distinction discussed in chapter 2. Task knowledge interacts with more general knowledge of expertise to link knowledge to context.[9]

So why do I use the acronym TAP instead of TEP? The answer is an example of frame changing on my part. Due to my background as a researcher with an interest in expertise movement in teams, I naturally gravitated to a focus on expertise and found Brandon and Hollingshead's description fitting. However, as I began spending more of my time working directly with senior decision-making groups in organizations, I came to realize that the term *ability* is more inclusive and meaningful than the term *expertise* for most leaders. Ability captures not just what someone knows (including their expertise) but also how capable they are at developing new skills, how flexible they are at adjusting to new situations, and how skilled they are at acting based on knowledge. All of these qualities are essential when trying to link a person to a task. This led me to shift my own translation of the research toward ability rather than expertise.

Two TAP Applications

In this chapter, I describe two applications of the TAP framework: the TAP Check and the TAP Team Expertise Assessment.

> TAP Check: The TAP Check is an easy-to-remember heuristic to use when creating a team or shifting tasks. It can take five minutes, and if it becomes part of a leader's routine, it can help the leader more effectively use available expertise resources.
>
> TAP Team Expertise Assessment: The TAP Team Expertise Assessment is a customized snapshot of team-relevant expertise. It is valuable as a tool to help a continuing team develop its members' expertise and improve its effectiveness over time.

TAP Check

How do you select people for a team?

When I ask this question, people often say something along the lines of, "Well, I try to find the people that have the right capabilities for the team or task." The reality is often not that simple. Managers may have people whom they want to train; the best people may be busy; there may be people who need work to do; managers may not even be sure of the needed skills, and so on. Reality is a place of imperfect information and imperfect matching of people and needed abilities.

In order to best use available expertise, a leader must know what people are good at, what expertise is needed for the task, and who is interested in developing new expertise, so that they can develop their team. Unfortunately, if leaders never consider ability in the first place, they never get to the conversation about who the right people are or even who the people are that the leader could develop through inclusion on a team.

My conversations with team leaders led me to conclude that we don't ask the question about abilities enough when we lead teams. Research has demonstrated that awareness of team expertise resources does improve team member performance. Changing the standard questions from, "What's the task?" and "Who are the people?" to "What's the task? What ability is needed?" and "Who are the people who have that ability?" will improve team performance if asked every time the team faces a new task—not just when they form a team. TAP Check provides an easy-to-remember framework for doing this.

- Step 1: Clearly define the team's task. Include any subtasks or execution requirements in the task definition.
- Step 2: Generate a list of abilities that are either (1) required in order for the team to compete the task, or (2) desired in order for the team to more effectively complete the task. Sort each ability on the list into either the required or the desired category.
- Step 3: Identify specific people who possess the abilities. It is acceptable to name a person multiple times if he or she possesses more than one of the listed abilities.
- Step 4: If you are also interested in developing team member abilities, create a second list of team members who need or want to develop the identified abilities. You can use this list to pair those individuals in need of development with individuals already possessing that ability when forming the team.

See Table 6-1 for a sample template for the TAP Check.

The TAP Check is simple. Its insights may not be earth-shattering, but the exercise can force us to do something that we do not often do, yet know we should—namely, think about abilities and be explicit about why we create teams the way we do. This is something that can be done in ten minutes. You can do it during a commute into work or while assembling the initial project charter for a new project. I've found value working through these questions not just when forming a team but also whenever my team is starting a new project or task. It can be a fantastic opportunity to quickly reassess team abilities and force yourself to

Table 6-1 TAP Check

Task: _____

Abilities	Who is strong in this ability?	Who wants to develop this ability?

TAP Analysis

consider if and how ability demands may have shifted with shifts in task demands.

Even if the leader has no control over team makeup, the TAP Check is a valuable ten-minute exercise. If team leaders consistently check ability requirements with each new team task, they begin to see and document patterns. For example, multiple tasks may require an ability that is not available to the team. By documenting this with each successive task, the leader begins to build a strong argument for why the organization needs to either recruit for that ability or free up resources to train on that ability.

In addition, if there is an ability that would be useful, but the team does not possess it, the leader can openly address this deficit with the team at the start of the task. By discussing this team gap openly, the team is given permission to seek ways to deal with this ability gap and can take ownership of working around this deficit. This is a far better dynamic than one in which team members grow frustrated and cynical because they've been given a task without appropriate resources, and they feel as if the organization either does not see the problem or does not want to admit the problem.

While the TAP Check is a simple heuristic to use to quickly match abilities to tasks, the TAP Team Expertise Assessment is a more in-depth consideration of team skills and their distribution. The TAP Team Expertise Assessment is a direct translation of the measurement technique I developed to assess transactive memory as a researcher.

The TAP Team Expertise Assessment provides a customized assessment of a team's task-relevant knowledge and expertise and helps the team members understand how to use that expertise to improve team performance. This assessment has shown that a well-developed team expertise system in a team can significantly improve team performance and development. The TAP Team Expertise Assessment focuses attention on expertise relevant to team-specific tasks and explicitly links the assessment results with barriers and drivers of the team's task performance.

The TAP Team Expertise Assessment is valuable for any continuing team with decision-making authority. Some of the advantages I've found with using this assessment include the following:

- The assessment is customized to assess the expertise needs specific to the team's environment and task.
- The process requires a minimal time commitment by team members.
- The assessment is well suited for comparative analysis among teams.
- The assessment is ideal as a team-development tool because it links results directly to team tasks.
- The assessment focuses team members' attention on the unique skills and relationships of other team members.
- The assessment process increases team member awareness of potential team resources and weaknesses, thus improving team communication.
- The assessment establishes a benchmark and methodology for future team assessments.
- The assessment process is based on an empirically validated methodology and sound social science.

The TAP Team Expertise Assessment Process

Step 1: Identify the Top Ten Abilities Required for Team Success
Interview four to five knowledgeable stakeholders to generate this list. I often include the team leader, the leader's manager, and external peers who interact with the team. I try to limit the inclusion of team members to no more than two because it is valuable to get external views on needed abilities. It is not necessary to rank the ten abilities. The abilities should be identified in terms

that are familiar to the team members. It is useful to take some time to write definitions for each of the ten abilities to ensure all team members are assessing the same thing. In many cases, you may be in the position to identify the key abilities without conducting interviews. It may still be enlightening to ask a few people these questions to test your own assumptions.

Why ten? A list longer than ten becomes difficult to manage and can lead to lower-quality results from the survey because it will make the survey too time-consuming for team members. In addition, if a team is unable to prioritize ten abilities, it may indicate a team that is overly broad in its charter or is struggling with focus or consensus.

What is an ability? As frustrating as this answer is, it depends. It depends greatly on the role of the team and the work it does. For some cross-functional teams, general abilities of communication, business acumen, and project management may be the appropriate abilities to measure. For some product development or information technology teams, it may be appropriate to assess more specific technical abilities.

The example I will use is taken from a small management consulting firm. In this case, the TAP Team Expertise Assessment was completed by all fifteen members of the firm (see Table 6-2).

Table 6-2 Top Ten Abilities for Success (Management Consulting Firm)

Analytical Skills
Business Development
Design
Entrepreneurship
Online Marketing
Presentation Skills
Project Management
Remote Learning
Thought Leadership
Writing Skills

Step 2: Create the Assessment Instrument

Team members will be asked to assess four aspects for each ability.

1. Rate the overall expertise level of the team.
2. Rate the range of ability on the team. Is the expertise of the most skilled person on the team far greater than the expertise of the least skilled person on the team?
3. Identify the person on the team with the most expertise or skill for the ability.
4. Rate your own expertise.

Creating the instrument is easily done using online survey tools. For the third question (identify the expert), create a drop-down menu in the survey software, which includes the name of each team member as a response option.

Step 3: Administer Survey and Collect Results

Administering this assessment is easily done using online survey software. For this assessment to be useful, it is imperative that every member of the team complete the survey.

Step 4: Score the Team

There are a variety of ways to report the results, so I'll describe the less complex ones here. The scores that provide the most insight and trigger the most valuable team conversations are scores of team accuracy, team variance, and team consensus.

Team accuracy measures how much the identified experts on a team are, in fact, experts. Generate a group score comparing answers to question 3 and answers to question 4 to calculate team accuracy.

Team variance measures the range between most expert and least expert on a team. This can be done directly using survey results from question 2 or indirectly by using the self-report scores from question 4. If there is a discrepancy between those two questions, you can share that with the team and ask them to consider why that may be the case. Team consensus measures agreement within the team about where expertise resides.

Team consensus can be scored by generating a measure of agreement on question 3 across abilities. Question 1 can also be used to generate a score of perceived expertise level for each ability.

I was recently speaking with a chief technology officer (CTO) about an expertise inventory exercise (not done by me) that his team had just completed. At the recommendation of his chief learning officer, his team completed an assessment of their work-relevant knowledge. He told me his team found this to be an interesting and valuable exercise, but they were left wondering what they should do with the information.

This seems to be a common end point for many knowledge-assessment exercises. The exercise is filed away in a "nice to know but not going to change anything we do" drawer of team-development experiences—right next to those Myers-Briggs scores and the memory of that ropes course you did at your last off-site meeting.

Team expertise assessments can and should be much more than that. I use the TAP Team Expertise Assessment tool to drive specific team member behavior commitments. Regardless of the tool used, at a minimum you can use the data to identify essential skill blind spots.

Here is one way I use the TAP assessment results to start a conversation about ability needs within a team. I often create a slide similar to Figure 6-1, sorting team abilities. It is important for a team to see the distinction between an accurate and an inaccurate understanding of who knows what within the team. This is particularly the case given the strong research evidence that accurate transactive memory systems affect team performance.

Often, results about accuracy provide a useful way to discuss communication and work visibility within the team. Teams have inaccurate knowledge of other members' abilities because of the lack of opportunities to see other team members work. The distinction between distributed expertise (many people on the team possess that ability) and concentrated expertise (just a few people on the team have high levels of that ability) provides a snapshot of how the team's abilities are situated. One type of expertise is not better than the other. It entirely depends on the ability being measured and its role in the functioning of the team.

In Figure 6-1, I outline four categories of abilities and their implications.

Figure 6-1 Sorting Team Abilities

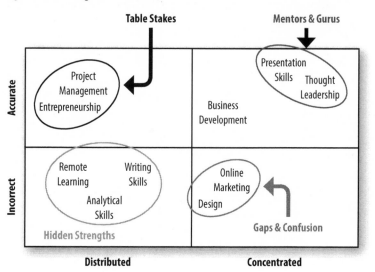

Table Stakes

These are abilities that are widely distributed across the team (virtually all team members are skilled at them), and members of the team—for the most part—know who on the team is most expert at them. These abilities are the table stakes or the money you need to put down just to play a card game and are likely the abilities that were needed in order to be on the team in the first place.

Table Stakes action: Ensure your team is actively maintaining these capabilities with periodic refresh activities or access to industry conferences/training. There is a risk that table-stakes abilities are deteriorating across the whole team if team members are comparing themselves only to each other.

Mentors & Gurus

These are the abilities in which expertise is concentrated in the heads of a small number of experts, and team members all have an accurate understanding of who these experts are and what they know. In most knowledge-based team settings (and this includes management teams), there is nothing wrong with such concentrated expertise because it enables efficient access to advanced knowledge. The obvious risk is that the gurus leave the team. Many of the highest-performing teams that I've had the pleasure of working with consist of one or two industry-leading experts and a larger group of intelligent, motivated individuals who extend the capabilities of the gurus.

Mentors & Gurus action: Tap into the gurus' knowledge and make them mentors for other team members. Pair the expert with one other person on the team who aspires to attain that same level of ability later in his or her career. In addition, ensure the gurus understand the need to remain accessible to other team members for knowledge sharing. In one high-performing team I worked with, one person was viewed as most expert on every single one of the abilities assessed. After further study of the team, I concluded this was an accurate assessment. I worked with that individual to develop plans to build the skills of different members of the team as either a mentor or by partnering with others on specific tasks.

Gaps & Confusion

These are the abilities team members believe are concentrated in a small group of identified experts, yet unlike the guru and mentor abilities, the identified experts are not actually expert. It may be the case that the expertise of identified experts has been overestimated because they know just a little more about that topic than everyone else does. These are the abilities that will prompt a team to assume the team has more capability than it really does. Unless the identified expert speaks up, this gap in team knowledge can remain hidden for a long time.

Gaps & Confusion action: The correct action for these abilities will need to factor in the sensitivity of the issues and the learning culture of the team. The team needs to confront the gap, but it needs to do so in a way that does not alienate the person who has been incorrectly assumed to be expert. The two most direct ways are to (1) make available training to bring the ability up to the needed level on the team, or (2) find a new team member who is expert in the ability. It is also possible that there is a hidden expert on the team whose capability is not widely known on the team.

Hidden Strengths

These are abilities that are widely shared within the team, but team members are unaware of who is truly expert in them. Many of us have experienced this dynamic. Think of those instances when your team was unaware of skills you had. This is more likely to happen if many people on the team have a moderate level of expertise in this knowledge area because they are unlikely to seek help and are more likely to try to solve problems on their own. In such a context, the team will never learn who truly has deep expertise in the knowledge area.

Hidden Strengths action: Institute a structured help-seeking process to encourage team members to solicit feedback even when they feel they can solve something on their own. This does not need to add time to a process, as it can be managed as a quick check-in. This small action will raise team awareness of hidden abilities and also improve coordination because members will have more awareness of what others are working on.

Knowing What Others Know

Awareness of who has knowledge on a team when combined with a team culture of helping and collaboration leads to stronger team performance. When you bring the right people into the team at the right time, you can go a long way toward becoming the leader in your organization who has the reputation for translating insight into action.

I've observed that knowing what others know has similar positive effects in top leadership teams. I was basing my belief on my own observations as I had not read research supporting the value of transactive memory systems in executive teams. Considering that I had previously done research on this topic, I think we can reasonably conclude that I may have been trapped in my own version of unquestioned brilliance. My prevailing mindset believed knowledge of team expertise drove executive team performance, so I looked for evidence that this was the case. When I found that through my experience, I grew more confident that my initial belief was correct, and I was heartened to read a recent study by

Heavey and Simsek validating my personal experience working with executive teams.[10]

In their study of ninety-nine small and medium-sized technology-related firms, they found a positive relationship between top management team-transactive-memory systems and firm performance. However, they found that this relationship was complex and strongly related to the top management team strength of external ties as well as the level of dynamism in the environment. For me, these findings reinforce the notion that the role of knowledge of team member knowledge is intimately tied to the context.

In more uncertain environments, knowledge of your team members' abilities will be more valuable if it is linked with multiple external relationships to help the executive team navigate their changing environment. Having the right people on a team can help a leader test mindsets, but it is the connections to people outside the company that help a leader see potential blind spots and emerging uncertainties. In chapter 2, I mentioned the old adage, "Hire people who are smarter than you." The research on transactive memory reminds us to also make sure everyone on the team understands in exactly what ways others on the team are smarter than they are as well.

GSO Decision-Making 7

The store of wisdom does not consist of hard coins, which keep their
shape as they pass from hand to hand; it consists of ideas and doc-
trines whose meanings change with the minds that entertain them.
—John Plamenatz

Common Sense That Is Not Common Practice

Leadership is about focusing and motivating a group of people to
move together in a specific direction. The ability to guide a group
toward a decision and generate buy-in for that decision is a core
leadership capability. I've been surprised by the number of senior
leaders I've encountered in global companies who seem to have
never developed this skill. Leader overconfidence has the unfortu-
nate effect of limiting options and marginalizing key team members during a decision process. In my experience, I've found that
most subpar team leaders are not being purposefully autocratic.

Most are simply not aware of the impact their actions have on their team.

Fortunately, it is possible to improve as a group leader and minimize the risk of slipping into the habit of inadvertently dominating team decisions. Every leader or prospective leader ought to have a team decision process that they use and make their own. It is not necessary to become an expert facilitator and learn a dozen group decision-process techniques. One just needs to find a single technique that fits his or her leadership style and commit to using it. As mundane as it sounds, becoming skilled at moving a group toward a decision while building group-member enthusiasm is the ideal way to stand out as a potential leader in any organization.

In this chapter, we will consider good and bad decision processes with an eye toward becoming better at seeing team dysfunction before it derails decisions. We will consider the use of sports teams as models of good team processes, and I will describe one pattern of facilitated group decision-making gone bad. I close the chapter with an easy-to-remember heuristic for diagnosing team decision problems.

In the left margin: Techniques for Transforming Insights into Actions

Four Core Roles of a Team Leader

A successful team leader is thoughtful about the processes his or her team uses to create, motivate, coordinate, and decide.[1] When a team is struggling, its difficulty can often be traced back to weakness in one of these four areas. Creating includes not just choosing who will be on the team but also how to reconfigure the team as tasks and membership change. Motivating requires balancing the needs of maintaining a team identity with individual focus on the interests and needs of individual team members. Coordinating involves aligning team actions with those of external stakeholders, enabling access to key information, and buffering the team from external distractions when needed. Deciding is using the team appropriately when facing decisions (every decision is not a team decision), making sure the team is moving forward through a decision process, and making sure there is follow-through once a decision has been made.

TAP (task, ability, person) analysis introduced in chapter 6 helps a leader with creating the task while also positively influencing team member motivation (by linking individual ability with team needs). The GSO (generate, synthesize, own) decision model introduced in this chapter helps a leader with the deciding task and, like TAP analysis, has a secondary effect on motivating. Stakeholder mapping (in the next chapter) helps a leader think through some of the coordinating demands of the team.

GSO Decision-Making

Team Decision-Making: The Good, the Bad, the Ugly

If you've spent much time at all working in an organization, you've experienced the good, the bad, and the ugly of team decision-making. When I ask my students to describe their best and their worst team decision experiences, they are able to quickly recall and describe those experiences. One goal I propose you set for yourself is to never be the leader that future executive education students will immediately recall when their professor asks them to describe the worst team decision processes. Aspire instead to be the leader remembered as part of someone's best experience.

The Good
Think of the best team you were part of and think about why that team was effective at making decisions. Some characteristics of these teams I often hear include respectful, fun, committed to the task, willing to change when a better solution emerged, open to new ideas, comfortable debating ideas, and eager to accept and support the eventual decision. Sometimes these teams are continuing teams, and sometimes they are temporary task forces that are brought together for a single decision. What these teams have in common is they outperform expectations, and they create deep commitment among team members.

It is hard to provide examples of good and bad team dynamics because so much of the detail is often hidden from the view of outsiders. Even retrospective accounts from participants cannot be fully accepted as truth, given our tendency to let outcomes color our memory. (Believe it or not, there were good points about that ex-lover of yours...and that championship sports team you were on in school was not as brilliant as you remember!) Having said that, it is still possible to learn from other teams' successes and failures.

Professional sports offer a unique opportunity to observe a good team in action as an outsider because so much of the team's performance is done in public. Obviously, there are private practices and travel time as well, but overall professional sports give us a uniquely transparent view of team process. However, it is useful to keep in mind that most team sports are not that applicable to the types of organizational teams most leaders are responsible for. Sports teams have some characteristics that are rare in other settings such as crystal-clear goals, a clear definition of who is in the team and who is outside of the team, and a coach who has been assigned with a single job of making the team as good as it can be.

Even with these differences, though, sports teams continue to be the most common types used as examples of great teams. Given this reality, let's at least make sure we use the right types of teams to learn from. Sports differ in their level of team member interdependence. Borrowing from the seminal work by sociologist James Thompson from 1967, Robert Keidel categorized these types of sports teams as pooled, sequential, and reciprocal.[2] I describe these distinctions to help you think through the relevance of using sports metaphors as they relate to your work teams.

Baseball and cricket are examples of pooled sports teams. These sports are primarily focused on the actions of one or two individuals at a time, and team performance is primarily the result of the aggregate performance of individuals. The game requires little in the way of simultaneous team action.

The strange case of unwritten rules in baseball: Baseball is virtually incomprehensible to people who have not grown up watching it. People in the United States would say the same thing about cricket. Baseball's incomprehensibility is certainly not helped by the bizarre assortment of unwritten rules to which players hold each other accountable. In short, any form of celebration on the field of play is generally perceived as "showing up" the other team and is grounds for some form of retaliatory action. This action usually takes the form of a pitcher deliberately trying to hit a batter. To most observers who are not players, it's easy to conclude that baseball players are particularly thin-skinned. This impression is strengthened by the observation that baseball players do not congratulate the other team at the end of a game.

The framing of celebration as showing up the other team illustrates the individualistic nature of the game. Though baseball is viewed as a team sport, at its heart it is very much an individual sport. At any moment in the game, it is a game that pits one individual against another individual: batter versus pitcher, runner versus fielder. When viewed this way, we can start to understand the truly personal nature of success and failure within the game. Every good hit is a personal failure of a pitcher; every strikeout is a personal failure of a batter. Celebrating on the field can be perceived as bad sportsmanship once it is viewed as celebrating at the expense of an individual on the opposing team.

American football is an example of a sport ruled by sequential interdependence. There is more coordination among players than there is in baseball, but the plays themselves are designed beforehand. If all goes well, each player runs a specific part in the play precisely as it is drawn up in the playbook prior to the game. Players need to work well as a single unit, but they also must be able and willing to follow the specific instructions provided to them by the coaches. Decision-making is hierarchical, and any deviation from the script is generally not well received by others on the team.

The jazz musicians of the gridiron: Although the design and rules of American football mostly fit the sequential category of team member interdependence, all players and all teams do not necessarily play the game that way. In fact, the best defensive teams in football often play in more of a reciprocal interdependence style. For these players, the game is more fluid. In 2010, I participated in a symposium with a number of professional and college football coaches who described the characteristics of their best teams.

Offensive coaches described teams that very much fit the image of a high-performing, sequentially interdependent team. The best teams were characterized as having better raw talent, an ability to execute plays with precision, and the intelligence required to recall a vast and complex collection of plays. Defensive coaches, however, described their high-performing teams in a quite different manner. The best defensive units reacted instantaneously to subtle cues from teammates, knew exactly how to improvise within their position and how it would affect others in their unit, and looked for opportunities to help their teammates. The presence of all-star talent was notably absent from the descriptions of best defensive units.

The impression this conversation had on me was that defensive units on football teams can play the game as a sequential interdependence game, but the best defensive units are playing a different game. These units are playing the reciprocal interdependence game. One coach put it best when he said, "My defensive unit is the jazz ensemble of my team. Their job is to start with an idea and turn it into something completely different by how they respond to each other."

Basketball and soccer are examples of reciprocally interdependent sports. All players are involved in all plays, and at any given moment, everyone in the game is mutually adjusting to the actions of others. To be successful, players not only need to be physically skilled, they also need to be perceptive about anticipating moves by team members and changing their play to fit the flow of the game.

It seems so simple: The National Basketball Association (NBA), one of the most team-based major world sports, is full of stars. It may seem odd that this sport is dominated by individual stars until you consider that there are only five team members playing at a time. Each player matters, and the impact of a single superstar on a team can be profound.

You would think it would be tempting for a team owner to just go out and recruit three or four of the best players at their position and proceed to dominate the league. You would be correct. This very thing seems to happen quite often in the off-season. These moves create a huge amount of press and build the enthusiasm of the fan base. Then, more often than not, the team woefully underperforms, the owner trades the all-star players, and for the next few years, the team struggles to recover from the financial hangover left by the all-star contracts. It seems so simple, and yet in practice it is quite difficult to make it work.

The 2008 Boston Celtics made it work. The Celtics had won more NBA championships than any other team in history (sixteen at the time), but they had fallen on hard times. The Celtics had not won a championship in over twenty years (1986 had been the last one). In the 2007 off-season, the Celtics owners decided to make a bold move. They signed two perennial all-star players, Kevin Garnett and Ray Allen, to join their current all-star player Paul Pierce. The result was better than even the most optimistic fan could imagine.

The 2008 team played to a 66–16 record and won the NBA championship. This represented a forty-two-win improvement over the 2007 Celtics team and the single-greatest team improvement in NBA history.

So why did this strategy work this time when it had failed so many times before? The answer is deceptively simple. The three all-star players committed to each other that they would do whatever it took to make the team successful. This meant that each of them would have to agree to change the way they played. Specifically, each one of them had always been the best player on their team for their entire career. They had always been the one who would have the ball and make the decision when the game was on the line. Now, they would have to learn to play a little differently and share the spotlight.

It is such an easy thing to say, and as an outsider, it is so easy to see that this is the obvious thing to do. Yet, think about how hard it is for you to change habits, expectations, and routines in your own life. Now imagine that for your entire life you've been told you are the best at what you do. Don't you agree it might be hard to change those habits just for the hope, not a sure thing, that it might lead to greater team success?

Interestingly, this 2008 Celtics team may have finally cracked the code for the league because in 2010 the Miami Heat followed the same script and had even greater success with it. In 2010, the Heat signed 2010 NBA Most Valuable Player LeBron James and all-star Chris Bosh to join their current all-star Dwyane Wade. The Heat then proceeded to make the NBA finals for the next four years, winning two championships. Time will tell if indeed the Celtics and the Heat cracked the code, or if the temptation of individual glory and fame will continue to get in the way of this "stack the deck" strategy in the NBA.

The message is this: choose your sports team comparison wisely. Autonomous decision teams and most senior leadership teams fit the basketball and soccer team model. Sales teams and some cross-organizational business development teams fit the baseball model of individual performers working together. Fewer types of business teams fit the American football model, which is interesting since in the United States football metaphors are probably the most common ones used in the business world. Complex-manufacturing-process teams, multisystems management teams, and some project management teams would be examples of teams that excel with minimal deviation from a design and strong hierarchical control.[3]

Another reason sports teams offer a valuable way to reflect on good team experiences, besides the public nature of their allowing vicarious learning, is that many people have experienced the emotional high tied to athletic achievement. It is valuable to consider how you can draw from that personal experience as a team leader. Mihaly Csikszentmihalyi called this emotional high and sense of intense focus "flow." Flow includes focused concentration on the moment, a merging of action and awareness, a sense of personal control over the situation or activity, a distorted sense of time (usually a slowing of time), and the sense of intrinsic motivation driven by enjoyment of the experience and process itself.[4]

Flow can also be thought of as a characteristic of a team experience. In this case, the aim of the leader is to create the context by working to make the process intrinsically motivating, clearing obstacles, and ensuring team members have the needed capabilities to thrive. In addition, team leaders need to recognize the flow dynamic and actively encourage the team when they sense the increase in energy and production that accompanies the intrinsic motivation of team flow.

Team sports experiences provide excellent source material for personal translation of good team dynamics for a leader. The experiences of intrinsic motivation and emotional high that athletes experience can provide the leader with a benchmark of what is possible when defining a great team experience. Of course, it is important to remember that it is unrealistic to demand or even expect a team to have a similar flow experience in a work setting. All the leader can do is create a context in which it is possible. The challenge facing the leader is to use the right source material for their own translation of good (is the type of team applicable) and to resist the urge to intervene when they see the team starting to ease into a team-flow type of dynamic.[5]

The Bad

I choose not to dwell on descriptions of bad team decision processes or bad team dynamics. I've found that most people can quickly identify and describe bad team dynamics by the time they are twenty-five. There is little point in dwelling on those in this book. Obviously, leaders want to ensure that they are not leading teams that will be recalled by team members as one of those bad team experiences when they participate in some future training course; however, that is a low bar. The better challenge, and the more difficult one, is to aspire to be remembered as leading one of the best team experiences a team member can recall.

Before moving off the topic of bad team experiences, let's consider what I consider to be secretly bad team decision processes. These are processes that seem to be well designed on the surface, but a peek underneath reveals nothing but team dysfunction. This is the decision process that is managed—perhaps by an outside facilitator, perhaps by the team leader—but does not actually help the team get to a high-quality solution. The team does reach a solution though, and the facilitator seems to know what he or she is doing, so people leave satisfied. This is a case of missed opportunity.

I developed a goofy way to describe a common version of this bad team-decision process. I recognize the hypocrisy of falling back on a tacky acronym when I've already publicly mocked an established and useful model of group development only because it rhymes. I have also quite frequently expressed irritation at the phrase "There is no 'I' in team," though in my defense, that is more because of my profound disagreement with the underlying spirit of the statement. Nevertheless, I offer up a cheesy mnemonic device of my own with no apology. Okay, maybe with a little apology.

*John's Facilitated Group Decision Process That Looks Great on
the Surface But Is Secretly Dysfunctional: The BAD Process*
B: Brainstorm. Sure, it sounds wonderful. Everyone gets to shout
ideas. Best of all, it makes you feel as if you are making progress, and the energy it generates is a positive thing. The facilitator
smiles inwardly at a job well done as the flip chart fills with ideas.

How can something that feels so energizing possibly be dysfunctional? First, let me make clear that all brainstorming is not
actually dysfunctional. When managed well, brainstorming can
certainly get the group decision process going and accumulate a
wide variety of ideas. Unfortunately, it is not often managed well.
An extroverted member of the team inevitably shouts out the first
idea. The extrovert is the person who builds his or her idea through
social engagement, refining the idea after first voicing it. Compare this to the introvert who may not speak until an idea is fully
formed. This means the first idea put on our brainstorming flip
chart is, in all likelihood, a half-baked idea, the idea that emerges
from the mind of an extrovert before it is fully thought through.

Once that idea is voiced, two cognitive dynamics take over to
influence the rest of the brainstorming exercise. First, the idea
anchors all subsequent ideas. A number of research studies have
documented the pervasiveness of anchoring in our sensemaking
process.[6] Once an idea is in our head, it will influence all subsequent thinking. The initial idea frames all other ideas generated
through the brainstorming exercise. Second, as much as we try
to give all ideas their due after a brainstorming exercise, we find
that groups give the first ideas on their lists more attention than
ideas listed later in the process. These two dynamics indicate that
a brainstorming exercise is at risk of being unduly influenced by
the ill-formed idea that starts the process off.

A: Argue. It seems like a reasoned debate about options, but
closer examination reveals some troubling dynamics. Individuals begin identifying with one of the options, and after a little
while, there becomes a growing sense that there will be winners
and losers in this debate. The group is unlikely to come to a consensus on a top option because the conversation is having the
effect of making individuals grow increasingly locked into their
initial choice. It may be subtle, but the group is settling into the

limited mindset-confirmation, bias-overconfidence dynamic. What is worse is there may be competing coalitions locked into this dynamic. In the end, the way out is through a vote. Some feel as if they lost, and the group does not end the process with a sense of fully shared ownership over the choice.

D: Decide. How can this be bad? After all, a decision is the goal of the group in the first place, isn't it? Actually, no, that isn't the goal, though many groups work as if it is. The goal is a high-quality decision, not just a decision, yet consider what often happens once a decision is made in many groups. It is checked off the list of tasks, and the group moves on. A high-quality decision requires something more from a group: a commitment to follow through and possibly even a commitment to revise to ensure it is the best decision for the context. Deciding can also be dysfunctional if it is reached at the end of a group debate that did not lead to resolution, and therefore the leader of the group or a powerful coalition just decrees a decision. The decision and the process leading up to it potentially damaged the ability of this group to continue to work together well going forward.

The Ugly

Don't worry, I won't spell this out like I did BAD. Ugly happens when team decision dysfunctions become personal. Ugly is when team dissention spills out beyond the team and infects other parts of an organization. Ugly may even make the news if it occurs high enough in an organization.

These are team decision-making dysfunctions that go beyond issues of having the wrong expertise or a bad facilitation process in place. They get into dysfunctions based on past interpersonal histories (I know not to trust him because he has lied to me in the past); misaligned personal, team, and organizational agendas (I am out of this crazy place as soon as I get a better offer!); and team members with poor team skills (not a "plays well with others" type of person).

The difficult truth is ugly usually cannot be solved by introducing a new process or calling in a facilitator. By the time we are to the ugly stage, resolution likely requires replacing members—with the team leader likely at the top of that list. A good professional goal is to ensure that you never let a team's dynamics get so toxic that the only way to fix them is to move you out of the team. The aim of providing leaders with decision-making techniques and making them aware of the fundamental leadership trap is to prevent ugly from ever happening.

The GSO Team Decision Structure

The GSO team decision structure is not intended to replace the many fantastic group decision techniques available. It is a shorthand way to remember what is needed for a group to consistently generate high-quality decisions. It can be used as a guideline for a structured decision process, and it can also be used as a tool for diagnosing where a team is having difficulties.

GSO stands for generate, synthesize, and own. Groups often struggle with some well-documented pathologies when attempting to make decisions together. Some groups never consider multiple options before settling on a solution (a type of groupthink); some groups are quite able to generate ideas but get trapped when trying to choose an option or prioritize (decision paralysis); and some groups are able to get to a decision but leave without full commitment to the decision by group members. These decision pathologies map closely to the fundamental leadership trap. Limited mindsets make it hard to generate strong alternatives. The confirmation bias leads a group to disregard the negatives of a preferred solution. Overconfidence makes it hard for group members

Figure 7-1 The GSO Structure

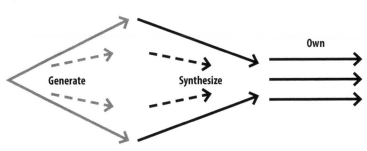

to build alternatives and sets up a dynamic of competitive options that are owned by individuals who are convinced they are right, as illustrated in Figure 7-1.

The GSO structure evolved as a shorthand way to help my students remember the key elements of a group decision process. GSO is an adaptation of the nominal group technique,[7] which does an excellent job enabling idea generation and idea synthesis to include the need to ensure that the group takes ownership of the next steps in the process.

Generate

Immediately honing in on a single solution is a significant problem for decision-making groups. It sometimes feels as if groups forget that their job is to find an optimal solution and instead act as if their job is just to come to a decision. This is understandable when you consider that many managers are pressed for time, and everyone knows that once the decision is made, the meeting is over. Overconfidence in the initial ideas can combine with frequent difficulties related to team-member power differences or conflict avoidance patterns to limit the generation of serious alternatives.

Indicators that the *generate* step is a source of team dysfunction include the following:

- Meetings consistently finish ahead of schedule.
- Some team members start contributing less and less over time. This may be a sign they've learned disagreement will not make a difference.
- The team has been "blindsided" by unexpected resistance to their decisions from those outside the group. This could be an indicator that options are not really being critically assessed.
- Team members enjoy working together, but the team is underperforming or feels underappreciated by outsiders—a possible indicator of a groupthink dynamic.
- For the leader, it feels as if most of the best ideas, or at least the ideas being adopted, come from you. Something may be preventing team members from offering competing ideas to yours.

The four tasks of the *generate* step are as follows:

- Clarify the question and check to make sure everyone understands it.
- Individually generate lists of options.
- Share lists and let others add to the individual lists (brainwriting).[8]
- Combine individual lists into a single list and check to make sure everyone understands each item.

Here are some facilitation tips to keep in mind during the *generate* stage:

- Do not assume everyone in the room knows that goal. Dedicate at least five minutes to making sure everyone has a similar understanding of the issue and what a good decision outcome would look like. I use a quick exercise in which I ask the group to identify decision elements that are in scope, out of scope, and secondary (choices that can be decided later), and I put this on a flip chart. If there are disagreements, the team leader agrees to go to the decision sponsor and get clarity before the team goes too far into the decision process. Most confusion tends to be around in-scope and out-of-scope elements. This is also an excellent time to discuss criteria for a good outcome.
- If the problem is ill defined, the group can still use the decision process to make progress on options. Go through the process of listing and recording options. Group the list of options into clusters of ideas that address different underlying issues. From this point on, treat the different clusters as separate decisions and go through the rest of the decision process separately for each idea grouping.[9]
- Don't be tempted to substitute brainstorming together in a full group for the individual idea generation. Individual idea generation is absolutely the core of this approach. It forces every member of the team to engage because no one wants to be the person who did not think

of at least one good idea. If you have a team of competitive people, they will fight for the floor in a group idea-generation exercise, but that competitiveness will be rechanneled toward their individual lists if they are given time to work alone first. In addition, individual idea generation will focus everyone on the issue at hand and increase the quality of ideas that come from the introverts in the group. Both of these approaches result in higher-quality and more developed ideas at the start of the process.[10]

- The process of swapping individual lists before the full group report-out allows the group to benefit from the variety of ideas that the individual generation of ideas offers while also taking advantage of the creativity that can be triggered through the social exchange of ideas. This is a version of what is often called brainwriting.[11] Along with improving the quality and variety of ideas, I've observed that this activity also begins to break down the sense of individual idea ownership and helps the group move more rapidly toward full group ownership of the ideas.

- It is possible to complete most of the idea generation prior to a meeting, which has the advantage of guaranteeing all team members will have already considered the issue prior to the meeting. When using this strategy, the team leader needs to be particularly vigilant that the team members have a similar understanding of the issue. One approach is to have a group phone call to discuss and define the task followed by individual submissions of options. At the start of the in-person meeting, the team can complete a quick brainwriting exercise, which will help everyone refocus their attention on the issue.

- When creating the final, combined group list, be sure to mix up the items so that one person's ideas are not all grouped together. The brainwriting will help with this, but mixing the list further will speed the process of having the full group take ownership of the ideas and reduce the tendency to try to guess the powerful group members' preferred options.

Synthesize

Decision paralysis often occurs in those groups that are skilled at generating ideas but simply do not have a defined process for coming to a decision. This can be caused by a number of things: a history of being criticized for decisions by those higher in the hierarchy, a lack of clarity around how to choose among options, individual blockers who simply refuse to consider alternatives besides their own, a risk-averse culture, or lack of accountability for action. We can sort these reasons into several buckets: lack of a decision process, a risk-averse culture, and difficult individuals (either on the team or higher in the hierarchy).

While the GSO structure can help with all three types of dysfunctions, if the problem is difficult individuals, a good decision process may have limited effectiveness. That difficulty may call for a deeper intervention. Consider seeking a leadership coach to help you manage that relationship or read up on some of the research that's been done on having difficult conversations and surfacing hidden conflicts.[12]

Indicators that the *synthesize* step is a source of team dysfunction include the following:

- Multiple meetings need to be scheduled for each decision. The team may be debating the same points over and over.
- Individuals are often unwilling to concede points or change positions.
- The team members constantly decide they need more information before they make a choice.
- New people are continually being invited into the decision process.
- There is a history of team decisions being unilaterally overruled by individuals higher in the hierarchy. This will create an overly careful team that will not stop until they have the perfectly 100 percent–defensible decision.

The tasks of the *synthesize* step are as follows:

- Combine similar options and rename them.
- Discuss each and every option with particular attention paid to discussing the pros and cons of each one.

- Rank or otherwise prioritize the options.
- If enough data are available, make a choice.

Here are some facilitation tips to keep in mind during the *synthesize* stage:

- Do not give any options a free pass. Discuss the negative sides of *all* options. One common block during the *synthesize* stage is when a member of the team has difficulty letting the team consider other options besides that member's favorite one. Do not stop discussing that member's preferred option until the group has identified some negatives of choosing it. A group member's passion for one option can be a good thing because it engages the group in the issue but only as long as it does not prevent the group from critically assessing the option.
- As a corollary to the previous bullet point, find the positives for each option as well. Occasionally a group member will get defensive when the group discusses the positive aspects about options other than his or her preferred one. As long as everyone understands that the process requires consideration of the pros and cons of all options, the discussion is less threatening and can minimize this risk.
- Before voting or prioritizing, consider the goal of the meeting. Is the goal to narrow a list to a smaller number of options? Is the goal to make a decision? Use your goal to decide how you want to do the voting.

Own

Owning the decision is not an explicit part of most group decision processes taught in business schools. The assumption seems to be that, once the decision is made, the situation passes out of the realm of decision-making and into the realm of execution or communication. This is a gap in these group decision models.

In practice, group decisions fail most often because of lack of follow-through. In my opinion, that is a failure of the decision process. Owning a decision means every member of the team, including those who had argued for a different decision, is willing to support the decision—in public and in private conversations. Owning a decision also means every member of the team is committed to moving the decision forward, either through vocal support of the decision to external stakeholders or through execution of the decision. Paying attention to the process during the *generate* and *synthesize* steps makes owning a decision easier. Specifically, confronting disagreements and noticing and acknowledging frustration within the team pay dividends during the own step.

Indicators that the *own* step is a source of team dysfunction include the following:

- Once the decision is made, team members disappear (don't initiate inquiries about the decision or are suddenly too busy to respond to team leader inquiries).
- Few on the team volunteer for the next steps after the decision is made.
- In your organization, it is not unusual to hear people discuss internal disagreement within their teams after a decision has been publicly announced.
- Your organization has a recent history of "passing the buck" and pointing fingers at others after public failures, creating incentives for team members to distance themselves from team decisions as a defensive mechanism.
- "Execution is not our job" is a widely held mindset in your organization and is often used as an excuse to disengage once the decision is made. If a team truly owns a decision, members will take interest in its execution, even if execution is not their job.

A leader can ensure a team assumes ownership of a decision by leading the team through a short set of questions. If any of the questions trigger warnings, the team can discuss ways to address the risks.

Questions to discuss as a team after a decision has been made include the following:

- Is there individual responsibility? Does each team member have a professional reason to take responsibility for this decision? This could be due to their role, their expertise, or an explicit statement by their supervisor assigning responsibility.

- Is there accountability? What happens if the outcome is poor or the decision is not executed? Do team members feel they will be personally accountable?
- Is there recognition? Do team members have reason to believe they will be recognized for a successful outcome? Will they be rewarded? Do they value the reward?
- Do they care? What would make team members passionate about the success of this decision? Why are they not? What can the team do to link the decision success to what matters most for each team member?

The GSO framework does not replace other, more detailed group decision models. It provides an easy-to-remember shorthand for remembering the three key elements of a successful group decision. Leaders can use GSO to diagnose team dysfunctions and help their team avoid the group-level version of the fundamental leadership trap. We may be notoriously good at persuading ourselves that we know more than we really do, but we are even better at convincing each other that is the case if we are not careful about how we manage our group interactions.

Stakeholder Mapping 8

We owe almost all our knowledge not to those who have agreed, but
to those who have differed.
—Charles Caleb Colton

Finding the right people and working with them does not stop
with the leader's team. Breaking out of the leadership trap also
requires an honest assessment of the broader set of stakeholders.
All too often, great ideas stall during the translation to action
because key stakeholders were missed or, even worse, avoided for
fear of what they would say. Avoiding consideration of a stakeholder during a change execution project because the leaders fear
the stakeholder will disagree with their plans is one of the more
common self-fulfilling prophecies I've encountered in my consulting work.

Often, when an internal organizational dispute spills over into
the public domain, it is the result of poor stakeholder management. A dispute may start when an initiative is designed with
minimal stakeholder input. Or little time may have been given

to stakeholder communication. Those are often the disputes that explode into public accusations, loss of trust, and stakeholder positions that become hardened by public statements.

Consider these two news stories that have all the characteristics of situations hobbled by poor stakeholder work.[1]

In the fall of 2014, eight of ten full-time faculty at the General Theological Seminary in New York City were dismissed by the board after they walked off the job in protest. This occurred after numerous confrontations between faculty and the newly hired dean over the course of a year.[2] Both sides vigorously blamed the other for the conflict as the dispute boiled over into the open. In early November 2014, seven of the eight faculty were reinstated on provisional contracts. It is hard to imagine such a vitriolic outcome if sincere stakeholder work had been occurring throughout this process.

In January 2015, Wet Seal, a teen-apparel chain, closed a number of its stores as it struggled to survive. Workers at the affected stores claimed that not only were they not notified that their stores would be closed (which is not unusual), but several claimed that the company lied to them about why inventory was being reduced at their stores and discouraged them from looking for other jobs (not usual and certainly not nice!).[3] Companies need to be careful how they communicate such news to employees, given the sensitivity of relationships with suppliers, landlords, and investors. In this case, it is also likely that Wet Seal's leadership was forced to take quick action on the store closings and was not able to give significant notice to employees. However, there is a difference between undercommunicating to employees and offering deceptive messages.

Power and Interest: A Tried and True Method

I debated whether to include stakeholder mapping in this book. After all, it has been around for a long time, and my adjustments to the basic technique are quite minor and more focused on how to use it effectively to uncover hidden stakeholders. I decided to include it for two simple reasons. First, for all its simplicity, it still improves virtually any decision or change process. I've been using stakeholder mapping in various forms in my facilitation and consulting work since 1994. Second, during the past five years, I have polled participants in my critical-thinking and decision-making executive courses, and I find that a vast majority of students have never heard of stakeholder mapping, and an even larger number have never used it. Those of us in the change management and organizational development field sometimes forget that even old techniques are new to most people!

Steps in Stakeholder Mapping[4]

My preferred approach to stakeholder mapping combines the power and interest grid with stakeholder salience. The power and interest grid has the advantage of being intuitive and quick, which is not to be discounted when one considers all the complex tools that are often being sold by change management consultants. The stakeholder salience framework begins the process of clarifying the different interests and needs of the high-interest stakeholders and is valuable when diving more deeply into stakeholder analysis.

Step 1: Draw the Power and Interest Grid on a Flip Chart (Figure 8-1)

Figure 8-1 Power and Interest Grid

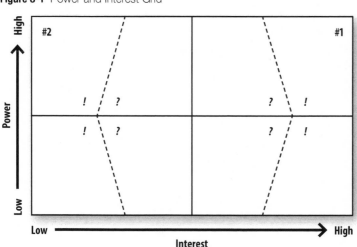

Step 2: Start by Identifying High-Power/
High-Interest Stakeholders

The meaning of high-interest stakeholders is self-explanatory. Remember that when we talk about power, we refer to power related to the success of the issue at hand, not just general power or authority. A stakeholder can also be an individual or a group. When identifying groups, take a moment to consider if there are subgroups that are relevant or individuals who should be pulled out of the group and considered as separate stakeholders. Place every stakeholder mentioned on the grid in the appropriate box, even those that do not fit in the high-power/high-interest box.

Place each stakeholder to the right of the dashed line if you have strong evidence of their interest. If you are merely assuming interest, but no one in the group has direct verification of it, place them to the left of the dashed line. This step is important because it is a check against the confirmation bias as well as overconfidence. Continue this step until no more high-power/high-interest stakeholders can be identified.

Step 3: Shift Over to the Left Side of the Grid and Try
to Identify High-Power/Low-Interest Stakeholders

Encourage people to name any stakeholders that come to their minds that are not already on the grid. As in step 2, place each stakeholder in the appropriate spot.

Facilitator Tips

Step 3 is the key step in this exercise. In my experience, asking people to think of high-power/low-interest stakeholders seems to flip a mental frame in people's minds. The result is that the group inevitably fills in the lower-right side of the grid (low-power/high-interest). Strange as it sounds, asking people to identify high-power/low-interest stakeholders leads to the generation of numerous low-power/high-interest stakeholders that were missed in step 2. These are the stakeholders that are essential to discover.

The stakeholders identified in step 2 were the obvious ones—the stakeholders that the team was already thinking about and the ones that, even without stakeholder mapping, the team was likely going to factor their perspectives into while making their decision. The stakeholders revealed in step 3 are the hidden ones—the stakeholders that would have been missed if the team had not done this exercise. The entire point of this exercise was to discover those stakeholders. They are the people or groups who have expertise or passion for the issue but are not in positions that immediately bring them to mind. Their expertise and interest may be valuable to tap early to improve the execution of the initiative.

Step 4: Identify Stakeholder Salience

Standard approaches to stakeholder mapping stop after the completion of a stakeholder map, such as the power and influence grid. Step 4 begins the process of building from the completed grid and draws from the work on stakeholder salience by Mitchell, Agle, and Wood[5] to start to tease out differences among the high-interest stakeholders. Add each stakeholder listed on the right side of the grid (high interest) to the first column in Table 8-1. Score each stakeholder along the three attributes of power, legitimacy, and urgency. I recommend a four-point, less-to-more scale. The four-point scale removes a midpoint score. It also avoids the tendency within groups to get caught up on precise numbering when faced with a seven- or ten-point scale.[6] I use the definitions of these terms taken directly from Mitchell, Agle, and Wood's original article, which they, in turn, drew from widely accepted definitions:

Power: relationship among social actors in which one social actor, A, can get another social actor, B, to do something that B would not have otherwise done

Legitimacy: a generalized perception or assumption that the actions of an entity are desirable, proper, or appropriate

Table 8-1 Identify Stakeholder Salience

Stakeholder	Power	Legitimacy	Urgency

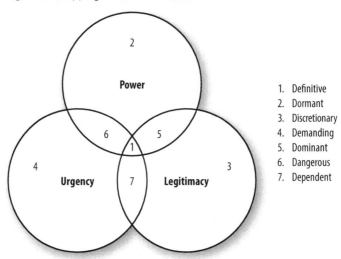

Figure 8-2 Mapping Stakeholder Salience

1. Definitive
2. Dormant
3. Discretionary
4. Demanding
5. Dominant
6. Dangerous
7. Dependent

within some socially constructed system of norms, values, beliefs, and definitions

Urgency: the degree to which stakeholder claims call for immediate attention

Step 5: Map Stakeholders Based on the Three Salience Attributes

Mitchell, Agle, and Wood sort and label groupings of stakeholders based on the degree to which they embody the three attributes scored in step 4. Figure 8-2 re-creates their suggested labels using a Venn diagram. Place stakeholders on the diagram. Scores of three or greater place the stakeholder within the circle for that attribute.

Next, I describe the stakeholder groupings using the titles given by Mitchell, Agle, and Wood; however, the descriptions are my own:

- Definitive Stakeholders: Stakeholders who combine power, urgency, and legitimacy. There is no doubt as to the importance of engaging and understanding these stakeholders. It is likely these stakeholders are obvious to most involved in the issue.

- Dormant Stakeholders: Stakeholders with power but little urgency or legitimacy regarding the issue. These stakeholders can be important parts of moving an issue forward, either by creating a sense of urgency or finding a legitimate role for them in the process. Dormant stakeholders are often targets for advocacy efforts.

- Discretionary Stakeholders: Stakeholders who have a legitimate interest in the issue but little power or urgency to act. These stakeholders can become powerful through organized action with other stakeholders. This may be more likely if they also see a reason to engage around the issue. Consider the example of current satisfied customers who learn that your company is considering merging with another in your industry. The customer has little power to influence the merger and may not currently see a reason to care.
- Demanding Stakeholders: Stakeholders who feel a sense of urgency around the issue but with little power or legitimacy. These could be outside activists who have a passionate desire to change the way an organization does business but have little current influence. These stakeholders often play an important role in crafting the arguments used by other stakeholders to influence the issue. Consider the consumer advocacy group that may want to block the merger of companies due to their concern that it could lead to higher prices and fewer choices in the marketplace.
- Dominant Stakeholders: Stakeholders with power and legitimacy. These stakeholders may not currently feel the urgency, but if they do, they can act in a manner that will significantly influence the outcome. In our merger example, consider the role of antitrust lawyers for the national government. Skillful campaigning by the demanding stakeholders could trigger action on the part of the dominant stakeholder to act. You can also create a new dominant stakeholder group through a coalition of dormant and discretionary stakeholders. For example, a set of key customers could convince a competing

company to act to block the merger through ties with regulators or through a competing bid.

- Dangerous Stakeholders: Stakeholders with power and a sense of urgency but limited legitimacy. These stakeholders care passionately about this issue but do not have a legal place at the table. They find their power elsewhere to influence the outcome. Consider how a consumer advocacy group could gain power to influence the merger. They could partner with dormant stakeholders, such as sympathetic lawmakers, or build a coalition with more powerful consumer groups. A large advocacy group may already have both power and urgency on its own. An example of this in the United States would be the American Association of Retired Persons (AARP). AARP's scale and political influence can place them in this stakeholder group on virtually any issue they choose to act upon.

  The name of this stakeholder group highlights how stakeholder-mapping work is also influenced by our potentially limited mindsets. These stakeholders may be viewed as dangerous to those who want to move the merger forward, but the very definition of who has legitimacy and who does not have legitimacy relies upon a specific framing of the issue at hand. It is healthy to ask yourself why you think a group does not have legitimacy and also to ask yourself who would disagree with you on this point.

- Dependent Stakeholders: Stakeholders with urgency and legitimacy but little power. These stakeholders are motivated to act but must form creative coalitions with others to have an influence. Their primary strategic aim is often to find a powerful ally to work with. An example of this type of stakeholder could be a state regulator who has no real power to block the merger but has the legitimacy to make recommendations and may feel some urgency due to the risk of layoffs in his or her state if the merger goes through. Lawyers who represent current customers could also fit in this group, if their power is limited.

Next Steps

The act of creating the stakeholder maps often clarifies the next steps, the most common of which include the following:

- Considering a stakeholder engagement plan: Which stakeholders should be engaged, when should they be engaged, and how should they be engaged? There are often one or two that could help the initiative most if engaged early and perhaps brought into the planning process.
- Strategizing the best way to frame the issue for stakeholders and ensuring the frames are consistent and aligned across stakeholder groups: Some issue frames may seem perfect for one stakeholder, but if used, they could turn another group against the initiative or even demoralize the change team itself.[7]
- Deciding how often to revisit the stakeholder work: All too often stakeholder mapping is done once during a project and then never revisited. Stakeholder dynamics are fluid and constantly evolving, so it is essential to revisit the mapping and make adjustments throughout the process.

Seeing the Hidden Stakeholders

The story of Branch Rickey and the Brooklyn Dodgers, which I briefly mentioned in chapter 2 and describe in more detail in chapter 12, is an excellent example of how stakeholder mapping can clarify priorities of even the most audacious and complex changes. By the beginning of 1944, Branch Rickey, the Brooklyn Dodgers general manager, had already decided to sign a black baseball player to play in Major League Baseball. He had the backing of the Dodgers owners, but other than that, he had done little to push the idea forward.

In the spring of 1944, Rickey began working with Dan Dodson, a sociologist from New York University, to map out a game plan for the change. The two of them conducted what today we

Figure 8-3 Stakeholders in Brooklyn Dodgers Decision

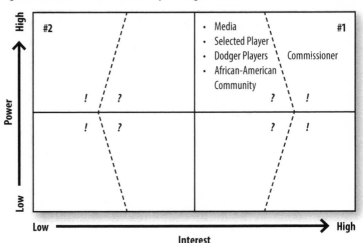

would call a stakeholder analysis. They identified five individuals or groups whose backing they would need in order to make the change successful. In their minds, these were the high-power/high-influence stakeholders. Figure 8-3 shows those stakeholders on our map. The five groups they identified were the Dodgers players, the selected player, the media, the commissioner of Major League Baseball, and the African-American community in Brooklyn. At this time, the only stakeholder whose position was clearly known was the commissioner of Major League Baseball.[8] In all likelihood, it was partially these discussions with Dan Dodson that led Rickey to conclude that the change needed to wait until the league had a new commissioner.

Rickey's subsequent actions indicate that he and Dodson worked through strategies for approaching other stakeholders as well. In the spring of 1945, Rickey had lunch with the highly popular radio announcer for the Dodgers, Red Barber. Rickey had no idea where Barber stood on this issue, and he also knew his support would be key to gaining the support of the fans. During this lunch, before Rickey had made any other moves and well before he had told virtually anyone of his plans, Rickey informed Barber that he planned to sign a black ballplayer.

By bringing Barber into the idea early, Rickey was able to mitigate the risk that he might block the plan and also seize the opportunity to get Barber on his side. In a subsequent recounting of this lunch, Barber reported that he was so honored that Rickey confided in him that he felt he owed it to Rickey—who was his boss, by the way—to seriously consider his position on the issue. I suggest that the Dodgers radio announcer is exactly the kind of hidden stakeholder that is revealed through a stakeholder-mapping exercise. These relatively low-position power but high-influence or high-expertise power stakeholders can make or break any initiative.

Understanding and Aligning

Stakeholder mapping can be a powerful way to limit our tendency to use limited mindsets and seek information that we are right. If we are not careful, we will find ourselves working only with those who agree with us and finding ways to avoid those who we fear may see things a bit differently. Such avoidance has the effect of increasing the sense of urgency felt by the stakeholders we leave out of our process. Our actions, or in this case lack of actions, may actually create new dangerous, demanding, or dependent stakeholders.

Stakeholder mapping is not about finding consensus. It is about finding understanding. We do not have to agree with the concerns of all stakeholder groups, but we will be far more effective in our efforts to create action if we understand their perspectives and work to align our efforts with those perspectives. Ideally, we can find common ground with other stakeholders. That will not happen if we do not make the effort to understand alternate viewpoints first.

Techniques for Sustaining the Action **IV**

Five men to twenty! Though odds be great,

I doubt not, uncle, of our victory.

Many a battle have I won in France

When as the enemy hath been ten to one.

Why should I not now have the like success?

—The Duke of York before the disastrous battle that leads to his

death in *The Third Part of King Henry VI*, Shakespeare

Sustaining action is a third idea translation. The third translation moment comes when it is time to take a successfully implemented initiative and apply it to another part of the organization or introduce it to new people.

The image that often comes to mind among managers is that of replicating. The goal is to replicate the success of the initiative in a new location. However, the image of replicating may be part of the problem because it is not a replication but a translation. The idea that was transformed into an action through the second translation moment is now effectively in need of another translation. In order for the translation be successful, once again the idea needs to be retranslated into an experience-near concept for the new context. To sustain action, this process must be repeated, over and over. Every new context and every new actor requires at least a slight modification to the idea.

Sustaining action is the poor relation of the three leadership translation challenges and is often ignored as a priority within organizations. It is rarely rewarded, and it is even more rarely held up as an example of leadership effectiveness. And, yet, if an action is not anchored within an organization's culture or repeated until it becomes one of the accepted routines within the organization, it will have virtually no long-term effect on the value of the organization. To be clear, here I mean "value" in terms of the organization's ability to achieve its objectives, not the far more limited and somewhat harmful definition of "value" often used to argue for the primacy of shareholder value as an organizational goal.

Dual head winds combine to make sustaining action difficult within large organizations: one is the significant amplification of the confirmation bias that occurs once an action has a record of success; and two is the lack of reward or credit given to those who are skilled at sustaining action. The issue of rewards goes beyond the scope of this discussion, but rewarding sustained success ought to always be a high-priority concern for any leader. Leaders get precious little acknowledgment for sustaining previous initiatives and significant recognition for successfully launching new initiatives. Is it any wonder so many organizations suffer from change fatigue? I will focus on the amped-up confirmation bias in this section.

At its core, the challenge of sustaining action is resisting the urge to believe that all the thinking and planning has been done and now all that is left is executing the plan. As the environment changes, so must the initiative. Sustaining action requires frequent renewal of the plans. The techniques in part IV can be applied at any point in a change process.

Sustaining action is always a challenge. For this reason, I view the three sustaining action techniques as the most flexible ones in this book. They revisit challenges outlined in earlier chapters but with a new focus on renewing momentum around an initiative. Though this redundancy makes these chapters shorter, so as not to repeat myself too much, it also makes these techniques quite valuable as a way to engage new people in a long-term change.

Tension Tracking $\quad$**9**

Do I contradict myself? Very well, then, I contradict myself; I am
large—I contain multitudes.
—Walt Whitman from "Song of Myself"

Going with the Flow

There are no steady states in organizations. I am always reminded
of the oft-quoted saying attributed to Heraclitus: "No man ever
steps in the same river twice, for it is not the same river and he is
not the same man."[1]

Many of the techniques we use to make sense of our environment are in effect snapshots that capture a single moment
in time within a constantly changing social system. Shortly after
we complete an uncertainty vector chart, the uncertainties have
already shifted. Shortly after we complete a stakeholder map, the
stakeholders have changed. This does not mean it is fruitless to

complete these exercises. That is like saying it is better to be blind than to have imperfect vision. These exercises help us make sense of our complexity. However, to be truly valuable, they should be revisited multiple times to chart changes in the environment.

Social systems are always shifting, yet we continue to rely on static plans and frameworks to design our initiatives. Our action plans, strategic playbooks, and annual goals seduce us into static views of the future. Sustaining action requires a leader to break out of a steady-state mindset and look for the dynamic tensions in the environment. These tensions are what will give direction to the important environmental shifts that will occur and are already occurring. Steady-state thinking is what leads to the proliferation of inflexible policies and strangely dysfunctional initiatives in large organizations. Something that in all likelihood begins as a sincere attempt to innovate or resolve a problem translates into a bureaucratic headache that does nothing to either fix the original problem or improve organizational goal attainment. I have never worked in or with an organization of over a thousand employees that does not suffer from this frustrating bureaucratic reality.

While it is tempting to spend time here debating why this occurs or how to fix it, that is unlikely to be fruitful, since this organizational tendency toward inertia has been with humanity as long as we have organized into larger groups. Let's start instead with the assumption that this steady-state planning is happening in your own organization and focus on how we can counter it as leaders. I focus on techniques that shift our attention to movement and change in the environment as a counterbalance to the natural default mindset of stability and a steady state.

Tension Tracking

Tension tracking is a set of questions designed to force the leader to seek and consider perspectives of other potential supporters and use that insight to initiate conversations with these individuals that will link the initiative with their challenges. The assumption is that each manager within an organization faces a different set of conflicting interests and goals (the tensions). The manager is constantly moving among these conflicting interests and mediating between them. A good manager does not get anchored in one position but is able to move back and forth between the conflicting interests. Tension tracking helps a leader consider the tensions facing a given manager and use that to help reinforce the desired behaviors. It is little more than an exercise in perspective taking with the operating assumption being that each individual faces different sets of tensions.

When sustaining action, leaders improve their effectiveness through their knowledge of other people's priorities and stresses as well as their knowledge of what makes each context unique. Tension tracking sheds light on the interpersonal element by combining perspective taking with the notion of a constantly changing environment. Most employees in a large organization find themselves constantly moving among the conflicting demands of different stakeholders. This is particularly true of those managers who straddle key boundaries within organizations. Some examples include sales managers who are responsible for meeting corporate targets as well as satisfying customers and a sales team, country managers who are responsible for managing a corporate brand and implementing global strategies while also innovating and competing successfully within a unique local market, and human resource managers who must maintain alignment with key corporate policies while also supporting and developing the diverse needs of different managers and markets.

The tensions that these managers, and others like them, experience do not leave them in a stable equilibrium position of nicely balanced forces. Rather they find themselves constantly pulled from one side of the tension to the other. Their reality is one of constant flux as various pressures ebb and flow. Tension tracking identifies these tensions and places your initiative within this context.

Revenue per Customer Versus Customer Centricity: An Example of an Unquestioned Tension

Many organizations have unquestioned tensions. I can state this more strongly. Most organizations have tensions that no one will publicly question or even acknowledge. These are tensions that are rationalized away by those within the organization as not really tensions. Outsider observers may see an obvious tension, yet organization insiders brush those outsider perspectives aside as ill informed or may even provide data to support their assertion that the two sides of the tension are not really in conflict. (Confirmation bias? Nah, not here!)

One such tension that is more common than many leaders like to admit is revenue per customer versus customer-centric service. Take the example of one of the companies you use for connectivity services. This could be your Internet service provider, cable TV provider, or cell phone service provider. Are you able to modify your service on your own without speaking to a representative of the company? What are you able to do on your own?

In many cases, at least with US service providers, you are able to add services but not remove services. In other words, you can choose to pay this company more money per month with a click of a button. No questions asked. Instantaneous service! If you want to pay less per month, you will need to speak to someone on the phone who will spend the next thirty minutes trying to talk you out of dropping services, or, even worse, you will be required to drive down to the local company store and spend a morning fending off hard-sell tactics in order to drop that service. Most of you reading this right now in the United States know I am not exaggerating in the least. This is an astoundingly anticustomer practice, yet these companies seem to choose not to see this and even market the convenience of their online customer service.

Why is this off-putting practice so common? It is actually an entirely rational way of doing business when seen from the perspective of managers within these companies. Revenue per customer is a very closely followed metric by equity markets when valuing companies. Since company share price is an important, if not the primary, metric upon which executives are evaluated, executives must use revenue per customer as an internal measure of success and reward managers accordingly.

Making it easy for customers to add services but difficult to reduce services certainly improves this metric. It is hard to argue with the observation that revenue per customer will likely go down if you give customers the ability to reduce service on their own. As long as your communications provider is trapped in the short-term shareholder value mindset of the publicly traded company, you may have to resign yourself to this unpleasant consumer reality. However, if you feel frustrated, imagine how frustrated the person responsible for improving customer service at that company feels! They are the ones who feel this tension every day.

I pick on communications service providers as an example because many of us experience this dynamic as consumers. The revenue-per-customer metric is prevalent in virtually all businesses. We train our sales staff to upsell customers, and we reward those people who are skilled at doing so. This practice is not inherently bad, but if leaders do not monitor it well, it can increasingly create tensions with other company customer service initiatives and goals.

Some companies have managed this tension by focusing more on customer retention than on revenue per customer. Of course, customer-retention metrics can create other dysfunctional practices such as encouraging long-term contracts that create a false sense of customer loyalty. What this illustrates is the more general tension between short-term profitability and customer centricity found across industries. Leaders can lessen this tension and get these two organizational goals more aligned, but they are unlikely to make this tension disappear entirely.

Tension tracking can help us better understand the shifting pressures others are experiencing within our organization. We become more effective idea translators if we develop a sincere understanding and appreciation for the other person's situation prior to any conversation we have with them. I often take this notion a step further and avoid starting a conversation with someone if I cannot think of a shared interest I have in common with the person. Engaging in conversation with a person with whom you can find nothing in common will not end well and will certainly not lead to any positive residual outcomes.

Recall the example of Branch Rickey's efforts to avoid engaging with the baseball league commissioner described in chapter 2. That is an excellent example of a leader resisting the urge to confront someone with whom he had little in common. Unquestioned brilliance tempts us to start the conversation anyway because we are certain we will be able to persuade the other person to "see things our way."

The leader takes a bit of a risk by initiating a conversation about tensions. The risk is that the leader may discover that his or her preferred action does not fit well within the tensions that are the other person's central concerns. The tempting action is to "pull rank" and demand the other person make your action a priority, which may result in short-term success and quick results but will not necessarily lead to sustained success. The risk is also that the leader may see something that he or she would prefer not to see—namely, that the action as designed does not fit the needs of the situation. Looking for commonality may lead to a subtle redesign of an action in order to create commonality. The risk is that the translation of the initiative into something aligned with local realities may change the initiative.[2]

Tension tracking is a short exercise to clarify the competing interests that are constantly pulling us, and others, in opposite directions. It is helpful to periodically examine these tensions in our own positions, and it is also helpful to consider the tensions faced by those who we hope will help us sustain actions. Tension tracking helps identify points of connection with these others (facing similar tensions) as well as potential points of contention. For example, your initiative likely contributes to one side of their competing priorities.

I will describe the steps for applying tension tracking to your own tensions. The same process can be repeated for any stakeholder, and I recommend doing so prior to attempting to engage them in a discussion about your initiative. You can do it quickly, perhaps on a commute into work, and the time is well spent if it helps you start the stakeholder conversation with an acknowledgment of commonality and empathy for tensions.

Step 1: Identify Key Tensions
Generate a list of tensions that pull your focus in opposite directions or that operate as competing interests when you are forced to make decisions. Start by thinking about decisions you make on a daily or weekly basis. When you cannot think of more tensions, shift your time horizon to a monthly or quarterly basis. After this, shift to a yearly basis and, finally, to a five- to seven-year basis. Table 9-1 gives examples of some common tensions, but these are just examples from previous groups I've worked with. It is quite possible that some of these tensions are not tensions in your organization. For example, I have worked in several safety-first

Table 9-1 Work Tension Examples

Quarterly goals vs. long-term investments

Global strategy vs. local market needs

Customer demands vs. team capability

Consistency vs. specialization

Safety vs. cost

Quality vs. speed

Fixing short-term problems vs. innovating for long-term improvement

Pricing/profit vs. volume

Work/life balance vs. demand to do more with fewer people

Revenue per customer vs. customer centricity

Manufacturing/service delivery vs. sales

Employee development vs. limited resources

companies where the safety culture is so deeply ingrained that they do not see a tension between safety and cost or safety and speed. The consistent, strong emphasis on safety has muted that tension within their culture.

Step 2: Identify Roles Connected with One Side of the Tension

Pick one or two tensions that consistently generate the most stress as you work to accomplish your objectives. Identify the roles within your organization (or with external partners, if applicable to your work) whose interests most closely align with one side of the chosen tension. For example, let's consider the global strategy versus local market tension. Global brand leaders or corporate executives have goals that are strongly anchored on the global strategy side of this tension. The country business unit president and the local sales and marketing teams have goals that are strongly anchored on the local market needs side of this tension.

Step 3: List Benefits of Both Sides of the Tension

Take the perspective of each of the roles identified in step 2 and list the benefits that are derived from taking that perspective. For example, if you focus on global strategy to drive your actions, you will emphasize knowing the benefits of scale, aligning marketing messaging, focusing investments on growth opportunities across markets, and developing global mindsets of leaders. If you focus on local market needs to drive your actions, you will emphasize customer needs, unique dynamics of the market, speed and flexibility in implementing corporate strategies, and the process for recruiting and hiring for deep local market knowledge.

Why focus on benefits and not drawbacks of each side? Our goal is to understand what drives people in a given role to prioritize certain tasks and discount others. We have a bad habit of seeing the benefits of our perspective and the drawbacks of someone else's perspective. By focusing on the benefits, we develop clarity around what motivates others, and just as importantly, we start to build a common understanding. By focusing on drawbacks, we frame the tension in terms of intractable differences, and we begin to subtly shift into an "us versus them" mindset anchored in differences.

Step 4: Connect Actions with Benefits
on Both Sides of the Tension
Examine your list of benefits from step 3 and make reasonable, realistic connections with the action you hope to sustain and some of those benefits. I emphasize "reasonable" and "realistic" because it is easy to rationalize causal links that are creative rationalizations but not real. Make a sincere effort to find the link between your actions and some of the benefits.

If you find it impossible to connect your initiative to any of the benefits on one side of the tension chart, this is a clear indication that your initiative is closely aligned with one side of this particular tension (for example, rolling out a global branding strategy is action that is sympathetic to the global strategy side of the global/local tension). If this is the case, you now have some clear insight into why and from where you will get resistance to this action. You can choose to modify your initiative to make it more balanced between the two tensions. Alternately, you can prepare your local leaders to address the conflict by openly acknowledging that this initiative is designed to address global strategy goals and prepare local leaders to openly discuss the tension inherent in the global/local competing priorities.

Techniques for Sustaining the Action

148

Perspective-Taking as Habit

Identifying new champions and supporters is essential if a behavior is to be sustained. Bringing in the support of new people is the only way any action in an organization will carry on and gradually become embedded within the culture. Expanding the number of supporters requires the leader to be strategic and thoughtful in engaging others. Each individual within an organization faces different challenges, different interests, and different sets of tensions.

Tension tracking as a technique is simple to explain and does not need a long chapter to describe it. However, it is worth highlighting with a separate chapter because it gets to the core of the sustaining action challenge. Tensions are fluid and always changing. The leaders' overconfidence that they have figured things out and do not need to continue to adapt the initiative, or that they already know what tensions a person faces because they have worked with other people in similar positions, is one of the greatest risks to sustaining behavior within a large organization. In short, they stop challenging their frames.

The HERE Snapshot **10**

The world keeps changing. It is one of the paradoxes of success that the things and the ways which got you where you are are seldom those that keep you there.
—Charles Handy, *The Age of Paradox*

First, Build a City

That was my first piece of advice to the US National Park Service. They had asked me how other national park sites could learn from the success of Golden Gate National Recreation Area's volunteer program. I said it jokingly. However, there is truth in the recommendation. If every national park had a metropolitan area of approximately seven million people, combined with a culture that encourages being active and civically connected, I suspect parks would find the task of attracting volunteers to be less challenging.

To be sure, other parks can learn quite a bit from the success of the GGNR volunteer program. However, it would be silly to discount the demographic advantage this particular site enjoys. Taking an initiative designed to fit this urban park and trying to make it work in Glacier National Park (located in sparsely populated Montana) does not sound like a recipe for success.

Of course, most contextual differences are not this obvious. We have to work harder to identify how one situation is different from another because we so badly want to replicate our successes that we are sorely tempted to discount the differences. This temptation drives us to focus on the great story of success and the specifics of the initiative that made it work in the previous context. Only as an afterthought do we examine contextual differences.

Countering this tendency requires us to start with a focus on the context. Only after a situational assessment is done honestly and vigorously do we turn back to the initiative. Consider the actions of most successful new leaders when they first step into a leadership role. The wise ones wait before making changes and force themselves to observe before acting. A submarine captain in the US Navy once said to me, "How can I know something is broken without first seeing it not work?" Forcing yourself to learn about the situation can help prevent the unquestioned brilliance that often contributes to premature initiative death. I developed the HERE snapshot specifically to create this situational focus prior to examining how to implement the initiative.

As with many steps in leading change, spending a little time up front saves lots of time and headache later.

The HERE Snapshot

Unquestioned brilliance is believing that your plan is perfect as it is and that any failure is due not to the design but to the execution. Obviously, this belief will only be stronger if the plan has already been successfully executed once already. In such a case, it is even easier to point to past success as evidence that current struggles must indicate a flaw in the local leadership team and not a flaw in the plan design. "If it worked there, it will work here" is a pervasive mindset. The HERE snapshot works as a counterbalance to this mindset.

Think about what goes through your mind the first moment you walk into a new situation at work. This could be a visit to a field site, a meeting with a new client, or the first meeting of a task force or project team. A natural reaction would be to make connections to your past experience: this client is similar to current client *X*; the vibe in this field site is just like what I felt at field site *Y*, and so on. In other words, you look for patterns and insight based on past experiences. I suggest that this natural tendency to look for similarities with your experience sets you up to slip comfortably into the fundamental leadership trap. If you look for similarities, you will find them. When you find them, you will grow more confident that you understand this new situation. In this situation, experience shuts down insight rather than contributes to it.

Rather than looking for similarities, skilled leaders train themselves to look for differences. They train themselves to ask the question, "What is different about this situation?" rather than, "What is familiar about this situation?"

Having a framework for quickly assessing a new situation before attempting to implement a change is an essential tool for a leader. The key word here is *quickly*. Unfortunately, we often feel immense pressure to act in these situations, and this pressure short-circuits our efforts at situational awareness. The HERE snapshot is a framework for rapid situational assessments. It helps a leader hone in on the essential, unique attributes of a new context prior to taking action.

The HERE snapshot overlaps with some of the other techniques we've covered and is best viewed as a set of questions designed to get you thinking about the connection between the unique demands of a specific situation and a more general initiative you hope to implement. With the HERE snapshot, the situation is given primacy, and the goal is to identify specific ways the initiative will need to be adjusted to fit within the situation. The HERE snapshot very directly translates the initiative into something that fits the situation.

I created the HERE snapshot after conducting a survey of senior organizational change practitioners in 2013 and 2014. One question I asked these practitioners was to identify the single, most common reason that change initiatives do not succeed. The most common responses were lack of stakeholder knowledge, unclear goals, unanticipated shifts in the environment, and misalignments between the change plan and the needs of the situation.

The acronym *HERE* stands for helpers, end game, reconnaissance, errors. It combines elements of stakeholder mapping and uncertainty vectoring with success and risk-mitigation questions in order to assess the four reasons identified by the change practitioners. The end result is a clearer understanding of what it will take to translate the initiative to fit the context.

Helpers

The key question: Whom do you need to know?

The stakeholders change in each context. All too often stakeholder mapping is done only once during an execution plan and usually at the start of the translation from insight into action. Of course, stakeholder interests evolve over time and ought to be tracked. In addition, every new context has a unique position in relation to stakeholders. The helping part of the HERE snapshot refers to completing the stakeholder mapping exercise described in chapter 8 *as it relates to this specific context.*

Pay particular attention to two elements while doing the HERE snapshot stakeholder mapping:

1. Map individuals—not groups—when completing the stakeholder map. Our aim is specificity. At this level of

analysis, a leader should be able to identify the relevant individuals. If the team cannot do this, the team needs more local expertise.

2. Pay particular attention to those stakeholders whose views are not known but assumed. Focusing on these stakeholders goes a long way toward countering confirmation bias and lessens risks that these assumptions remain untested.

End Game

The key question: What does success look like *here*?

Change management experts place significant importance on communication efforts for organizational changes. All too often, this recommendation is translated into a specific task given to the organization's human resources department, and those professionals are asked to create the communication strategy for a change initiative. The end result is a set of general messages explaining the value of the initiative provided to managers to help them execute the change in their area. The end-game step in the HERE snapshot starts by tossing those messages out the window. Okay, so that is an overstatement. In reality, we do not ignore these top-down messages, but we do need to accept that they are written by people who have a deep understanding of the initiative but may very well have a limited understanding of your specific context.

End game is about translating general statements about the goals of the change into more specific statements about what the future looks like in this local environment if the change is successful.

The end-game question: One day in the future, you arrive at work, and it is clear that this initiative has been completely successful. Describe that day. Be specific about what is different and how things have improved. For whom have situations improved?

By describing the future in specifics, we take advantage of the power of stories to help translate a general idea into a contextually relevant idea. Once the end goal of the initiative is translated into a local success story, it starts to have local ownership and feels less like an outside idea being forced on local participants. As with any idea translation, it is likely that the initiative is subtly changed when described in terms of local success.

Reconnaissance

The key question: What can't you know?

Reconnaissance is about turning your focus to the key uncertainties. To do this rapidly, complete a PEST+ analysis of the situation. Recall PEST+ is the first three steps of the uncertainty vectoring technique from chapter 4. At a minimum, you need to identify, categorize, and prioritize the top uncertainties. If there is time, identify how to monitor those uncertainties as well.

Those who participate in a PEST+ exercise become more attuned to the uncertainties in their environment. It does not matter if a PEST+ analysis was completed during the initiative design stage, as it is different when completed by new people and in a new context. Highlighting that which is not known, particularly when done with key stakeholders (identified in the helper step) and after success has been defined (the end game step), goes a long way toward reducing overconfidence and orienting the implementation team on the specifics of the situation.

Errors

The key question: Where are you wrong?

There is only one certainty about an execution plan: it is wrong. As noted in chapter 1, we make our plans at the time when we know the least about the world—at the beginning of the process. Even the most brilliantly designed plans will include some assumptions about the environment that will turn out to be incorrect. All plans are wrong. Skilled leaders accept this, and rather than spending their time trying to design perfect plans and fighting to force the world to fit into them, they spend their time monitoring for misalignments and adjusting the plan on the fly to account for these design errors.

While it is not possible to predict all errors in the plan (as the plan would have done so and been a different plan!), it is possible to anticipate some critical risks and assumptions that may determine success or failure. Once we've completed the helper, end game, and reconnaissance steps, we are in a good position to anticipate potential ways our plan may be wrong in this specific context. The error step takes the insights from the first three steps and builds a flexible monitoring plan around them.

Once you've worked through the HERE questions, design a plan to monitor pivot points, core assumptions, and key participants.

The HERE Snapshot

Pivot Points

    1a. Identify key pivot points in your plan. Pivot points are those moments that will determine if your initiative jumps over to a path leading to failure or continues on a path toward a successful outcome.

    1b. For each pivot point, identify the early warning signs that may indicate the initiative is off track.

    1c. Identify one or two mitigating actions the team can take to keep the initiative on track.

    1d. Assign ownership of monitoring this to individual members of the implementation team.

Core Assumptions

    2a. Which of the uncertainties listed in the reconnaissance step are most uncertain? In other words, which are the hardest to predict with certainty?

    2b. How will this uncertainty affect the initiative?

    2c. How are you monitoring this uncertainty?

    2d. Assign ownership of monitoring this to individual members of the implementation team.

Key Participants

    3a. Which key stakeholders do you know the least about? What role will those stakeholders play in implementing this initiative?

    3b. What would you wish to know about them?

    3c. How will you get that information?

    3d. Assign ownership of engaging with these stakeholders to individual members of the implementation team.

Keeping the First Success in Perspective

As I discussed in the first chapter, researchers have found evidence that individuals actively prioritize data that suggest they are correct.[1] One of the biggest difficulties with sustaining an initiative is that we assume the initial success is replicable. The confirmation bias prompts people to look for evidence that their plan will work and to discount evidence that their plan will not work. When it comes to applying new ideas and initiatives in a new context, the confirmation bias research warns us that we will look for the similarities among the contexts and use those as an argument that the idea will work. At the same time, we may discount the differences among the contexts. This can lead to an automatic application of the idea and subsequent surprise when the idea doesn't work as well in the new context.

When the initiative fails in the new context, it is tempting to blame the execution. Since the idea worked in the first context, if it didn't work in the second context, observers can easily blame poor execution. It does not help that we reward our leaders for successful outcomes of pilot projects, not successful learning from pilot projects. This creates a temptation to run pilots in initiative-friendly contexts rather than in challenging or even representative contexts.

Inwardly focused planning processes can contribute to this desire to find evidence that the plan should work elsewhere. Good global marketers have learned that it is a mistake to try to simply sell a product designed for one market in another market without attempting to understand the characteristics of the customers in the new market.[2] In much the same way, shifting an initiative to a new part of an organization requires an understanding of the characteristics of that part of the organization. Unfortunately, initiatives are often designed within the central corporate culture of an organization and imposed on the peripheral units. Efforts to question the initiative or to challenge its design may be viewed as resistance to change and not taken seriously.[3]

The hero who successfully led the first pilot of the initiative may have unrealistic expectations for what it will take to persuade a new group of people. Much as the sudden transformation that occurs during the first eureka moment can lead to unrealistic expectations of the time needed to translate it to action, the need for an idea champion to maintain momentum and energy during initial stages can become an impediment when trying to sustain the change. The success experienced by the idea champion during the first attempt to execute the idea can lead to the overconfidence that makes it difficult for the champion to see the potential blind spots when the context is shifted. The previous success at overcoming barriers can lead to a misinterpretation of the idea's fit with the new context.

One study found that ideas that were championed by an individual were characterized as being faster to decision but less likely to be implemented than were ideas that were decided through a more shared bargaining process.[4] When shifting an initiative to a new context, the previous success may limit the use of bargaining as part of the process. Thus, engagement of stakeholders may not be as natural as it would be during a process without a natural idea champion. Once again, misalignment may be seen as resistance to change.

Catching Our Unquestioned Brilliance before
It Becomes Unquestionable Failure

I've run the HERE snapshot exercise with executives from a range of organizations, including large consulting firms, energy companies, government regulatory agencies, and nonprofit organizations. In every case, the exercise revealed unquestioned assumptions and blind spots in current initiatives. We uncovered missing stakeholders, questionable assumptions, dangerous uncertainties, and exciting images of what success looked like.

All too often, we enter new situations with the assumption that the plan is right, and we look for evidence of this. When we get pushback from others that the plan "will not work here," we interpret that pushback as resistance to change or, worse, incompetence. The HERE snapshot helps refocus our attention on the needs and unique aspects of the situation and away from our unquestioned belief that the initiative is perfect as it is.

Reverse Default Setting 11

The snake which cannot cast its skin has to die. As well the minds which are prevented from changing their opinions; they cease to be mind.
—Friedrich Nietzsche

Where's My Fork?

When you travel to another country, what is your expectation? Do you assume things will be mostly familiar to you or do you expect differences? Do the differences stress you or make you uncomfortable? How do you react to these differences? Do you seek out familiarity? Do you dive in and try to experience more of the differences?

I travel quite a bit for my work, and I've always been fascinated by the different default assumptions that other travelers make. We all fall back on defaults easily when faced with something new.

Defaults are comforting. When the default option is not available, we can quickly get confused. We become like the US tourist I overheard while eating dinner at a restaurant in Beijing—a restaurant with mostly local customers—who asked "Where's my fork?" in a confused tone when his food arrived. Chopsticks were definitely not on his mind when he signed up for the trip to China. Assuming others eat the way you do and conform to similar norms of dress, conversation, and etiquette are all examples of default assumptions we all have until we travel to another part of the world.

Of course, not everyone falls back on their defaults so quickly when traveling. Perhaps you do not venture far from your hotel or stick with well-known tourist group tours when traveling in new places. Alternately, perhaps you are someone who seeks experiences outside of the standard tourist or business traveler experiences.

The Najafi Global Mindset Institute at Thunderbird School of Global Management has done some fascinating research on individual differences related to embracing what they call a leader's global mindset.[1] They define a global mindset as a set of individual attributes that help influence individuals, groups, and organizations that are unlike the leader's. Three groupings of attributes contribute to a person's global mindset: intellectual, emotional, and social. Intellectual capital includes concepts such as cognitive complexity, global business savvy, and a cosmopolitan outlook. Emotional capital includes items such as quest for adventure, passion for diversity, and self-assurance. Social capital includes intercultural empathy, interpersonal impact, and diplomacy, for example.[2]

I would make the argument that individuals who score highly on these attributes are individuals who have cultivated a skill and interest in breaking out of their default assumptions. They seek out difference. They thrive on surprise and adventure. Reverse default setting is a technique that can help trigger the sense making that comes naturally to these global adventurers among us.

The recurring theme of the chapters in part IV is that success drives an expectation of further success. Not only do we expect past successes to be easily replicated in new settings and over time, but we also expect past successes to inherently inspire others to accept and adopt the initiatives. We can find ourselves shocked when others do not adopt these actions, which to us seem clearly superior to the old way of doing things.

What we may be missing is that our desire to see our actions as successful may be leading us into a causal bias. In other words, we may see a cause-effect relationship between our initiative and success where it does not exist, and even if such a relationship does exist, others may not see it as clearly. Causal bias is in some ways a form of confirmation bias. We look for evidence of causal patterns that we expect to see, and we may discount other aspects of statistical relationships that muddle or even fully contradict the expected causal relationship.[3]

Errors in assessing causal relationships emerge from our desire to see patterns and explain our environment but also from the nature of causality as something that must be inferred from our observation and data rather than something that can be directly observed.[4] Thus, framing effects and confirmation biases take their place front and center in our sense making when confronted with questions of causality.

The good news is that developing critical-thinking competencies by training people to consider base rates and ratios when assessing data can potentially reduce the causal bias.[5] The bad news is that in cases where individuals have an ideological belief system that creates a strong desire for one type of causal relationship to be true, critical-thinking training may actually strengthen the causal bias!

In a series of intriguing studies and articles, Dan Kahan of Yale University and his colleagues found that increases in scientific literacy and numeracy led to greater polarization of viewpoints rather than greater consensus on the issue of climate change. In short, individuals use their information-processing ability to maintain the mindsets that keep them loyal to the affinity groups with whom they identify.[6] This research is relevant and has potential implications for assessing causality of organizational actions. Managers have significant motivation to find success and may even have their personal identities tied up with the success or failure of their initiatives. Combine this individual desire to see success with the strong shared belief systems that often permeate industries, and you may have a context that encourages the type of motivated reasoning described by Kahan.[7]

Reverse Default Setting

What If You Are Wrong?

This is the closing question I challenge you to consider. I debated what I should include in this book as my final technique because evidence indicates that we tend to remember the last thing we read, if it is distinct enough.[8] Some other provocative research on ranked lists reminds us that we rather mindlessly pay more attention to items in the 10th position when confronted by rankings.[9] Though I am not ranking these techniques, this research comes to mind given my central concern about actively challenging unquestioned biases as I describe this 10th technique. Initially, this led to my overthinking things a bit, so I simplified it by asking myself the following question: what is the one quick action a leader can take that can keep an initiative on track, even as the world around him or her is changing? Reverse default setting is my answer.

For any given situation, you have an assumed default prediction—the way you expect events to play out. Your default prediction is your starting mindset, and like any limited mindset, it is derived from your experience, your perception, and your hope. Because this is your default option, you will naturally seek evidence supporting it without giving too much thought to it. Recall the example of guessing my college sport from chapter 1. You sort and weigh data based on what you believe to be true.

The default is what we assume or what we do if we do not think about it. It is where our inertia leads us. If you refer to the list of techniques at the end of chapter 2, you will see that I say that reverse default setting takes only ten minutes. That may even be an overstatement. I often do it in one to two minutes when I am traveling somewhere. It comes down to four steps: identify your default prediction, consider the implications if you are wrong about that prediction, design at least one question you will ask when you step into the situation to test your assumption, and identify early warning signs that will indicate your default prediction is incorrect.

Step 1: Define Your Default Setting

Consider the question, "What do I expect will happen?" to explicitly reveal and define your default. Every situation has a default expectation. Some common ones include the following:

- You expect to succeed.
- You expect a certain person or group of people to be resistant.
- You expect to enjoy yourself (or alternately you expect to be bored/frustrated/disappointed/something else).
- You expect to be able to finish your task.
- You assume you have all the information you need.
- You anticipate a clear outcome (that is, it will be clear that you succeeded or failed).

Once you've identified a default prediction, define the assumed outcome more specifically. What does success look like? What would resistance look like?

Step 2: Reverse Your Default

The question driving this step is this: what if your default-assumed outcome turns out not to be true? Consider what that would look like. How would outcomes be different? Would different stakeholders be involved? What are some reasonable trigger events that could shift reality into this nondefault future?

Step 3: Design a Question to Test Your Default Assumption

What question can you ask that will help you test your assumption, and whom will you ask? We often enter new situations and, without thinking, identify how the situation is similar to other situations we've experienced because we naturally look for similarity and familiarity. We lean on our experience to make sense of the situation, which also means we are primed for the confirmation bias. If we look for similarity, we will find it, thanks to our well-developed ability to find patterns in any context. However, step 2 and step 3 reverse this tendency. Before slipping into the routine of looking for similarity, we train ourselves to look for differences. Asking how things could turn out to be not as expected is one way to break this routine.

When I step into an executive training session, I first look for something surprising. I've likely taught the content hundreds of times. I may have even taught in the same room dozens of times, so it is easy to see the familiar. These are the situations in which it is most important to remember reverse default setting. These are the situations in which you will find yourself blindsided by something unexpected.

Step 4: Identify Early Warning Signs

Step 2 and step 3 shift you into active processing mode. Hopefully, this inquiry reveals something new—potentially something that challenges your assumption about a default outcome. Now identify things to monitor to keep you honest moving forward. What are the early warning signs that the world may not be moving toward the default-predicted outcome? How will you track those signs? How often will you check them?

Short, Simple, Valuable

This is by far the shortest chapter. This is also by far the easiest technique to build into your daily routine. Building a habit of asking "What is different here?" and "What would prove me wrong?" may be one of the most powerful ways to keep yourself out of the fundamental leadership trap. You can start practicing this immediately in your next meeting. Do it often enough, and it will become second nature. In addition, you may suddenly find yourself noticing things about your colleagues, your clients, and your surroundings that you had never noticed before.

Questions that focus our attention on difference, uncertainty, and error weave through all the techniques in this book. Reverse default setting simply reduces the technique to the question, which is similar to the premortem exercise described by Gary Klein.[10] In a premortem, participants set themselves in the future and assume their project was a failure. They then consider how that could have happened. What did they miss? What went wrong? This exercise stress tests a decision or a project before launch. It makes participants look for blind spots and address them before they can derail the project. Another example of this is scenario planning as described by Paul Schoemaker.[11]

Actively looking for alternate perspectives as a standard part of any process is another habit that pays quick dividends. Procter & Gamble developers, engineers, and managers observed or interviewed more than a thousand customers before designing

166

their razor for the Indian market.[12] This required a starting point of accepting that they (the executives) may not know enough about shaving habits of Indian men and a commitment to action to address that gap in knowledge prior to designing a razor. The commitment to acting on the insight is as significant as is looking for the insight in this story. Procter & Gamble's effort to understand the mindsets of their potential customers had a side effect of providing data to counter the confirmation bias.

It all starts from an admission that you simply may not know what an alternate frame may be. Such an admission need not paralyze you. If done well, it does not slow you down; in fact, it will anchor your action in reality. The simple act of questioning your default setting and acting on that insight can provide the needed spark to challenging your brilliance with your team. If you seek some more ideas on ways to challenge conventional thinking within your organization, I recommend Lisa Bodell's excellent book, *Kill the Company*.[13]

Remember, there is only one thing you know for certain about your default prediction about the situation: it is wrong! You just don't know what part of it is wrong yet.

Breaking Out of Routines **V**

Routines keep us in our automatic processing modes. Routines enable us to remain in our limited mindsets and not notice the ways we keep looking for evidence we are right. The technique or question that can help us break a team out of a routine and avoid the fundamental leadership trap will be different for each situation. You can draw from the techniques outlined in this book in your own unique situations, but it is a mindset of inquiry and creativity that can trigger the best insights.

In chapter 12, I describe a situation in which the architect of a bold change was able to succeed partially because he worked hard to understand alternate perspectives and address them *before* acting. It was the ability to see different mindsets combined with careful thought about stakeholders and his change team that kept the change on track. As with your own work challenges, most of the techniques described in this book do not match his challenge. There is not a routine to break out of routines, just a helpful menu of techniques from which to choose.

A Story of Janusian Thinking and Stakeholder Action

12

Creating Our Own Luck

In this chapter, I will tell the story of one audacious change attempt that was successful partially because the architects of the change questioned their brilliance just enough to keep the change on track as the world shifted around them. They saw opportunities others missed, identified blind spots in their plans before acting, worked to build a change team with the right expertise, built out a stakeholder strategy from the start, and quickly changed plans when it was clear the initial plan would not work.

I refer back to the actions of Branch Rickey and his work with the Brooklyn Dodgers in the 1940s. I've already used this story to illustrate points in chapter 2 and chapter 8. Here I offer a more detailed account.[1] This is not intended to illustrate everything covered in this book, but it is an application of the underlying ideas outlined in this book to a specific type of change process. Recall my point in chapter 2 that, for most initiatives, only a few techniques offered here may be appropriate. Your job as a leader is to find the ones that fit your situation.

Change from the Top

The CEO of an energy company once told me of his frustration with his industry and his company. He saw an urgent need to develop multiple alternative energy resources. On a personal level, he saw this need as an ethical issue of global stewardship, while, as an executive, he saw the shift toward renewable resources as essential for the long-term sustainability of his company. However, the pressure to maintain growth, meet shorter-term financial objectives, and not "rock the boat" of industry solidarity made it difficult for him to initiate strategic change in this key area.

We sometimes assume those at the top of an organization have the capability to initiate and carry out successful strategic change because of their positions. This assumption fails to recognize that organizational leaders are constrained by organizational and environmental expectations as well as by perceptions about the types of actions that are legitimate for people in their position. Furthermore, we must recognize that the power of these leaders is often derived from the status quo, and any significant social reordering may undermine their base of power. Often, these leaders are caught in the bind of radical expectations. Activists (and this can include stockholders) can't understand why the organizational leaders don't act, while the leaders struggle to bring their actions on behalf of the organization in line with their own values and standards.

Leading change in organizations is a difficult and politically dangerous balancing act. These risks increase in *controversial strategic change*—change that challenges deeply held organizational norms and perhaps even broader social norms.[2] Tradition and history strengthen resistance to the change at the individual, organization, and industry levels. Some examples of social issues that have prompted strategic changes within business organizations over the years include environmentalism, civil rights, gender equality, and domestic-partner benefits for gay employees. In each of these issues, private organizations led the way by challenging social norms and redefining the issues. Strategic business changes that fit this category can include exiting markets, large-scale restructuring of supply chains, or merging with longtime competitors.

Figure 12-1 Framing during a Controversial Change Process

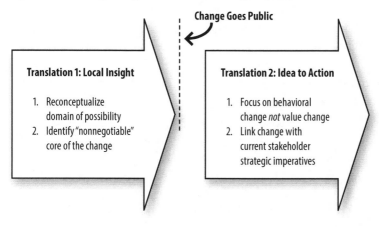

Even for those at the top of an organization, unquestioned brilliance can get in the way of a successful attempt at controversial strategic change. A controversial change of any kind will have greater likelihood of success if it is carefully framed and planned to fit within the existing value structures of the organization and its environment. This entails translating a general idea to a local insight and successfully translating that insight into action. To the extent that the leader can balance passion and confidence in success with the active cognitive processing that reduces unquestioned brilliance, he or she can increase the odds of success.

When initiating a controversial change process, the change leader(s) has two essential tasks to complete before the change goes public (see Figure 12-1). First, the change leader develops an understanding of the change that connects the change with other legitimate strategies within the organization. This requires an ability to reconceptualize the issue and create new strategies linking the controversial action with other strategic imperatives. Second, the change leader identifies the "nonnegotiable" core of the change. Institutional pressures will tend to rework controversial changes into less controversial actions. The change leader needs to have a clear understanding of the parts of the change not up for negotiation during this process.

Once the change is made public, the change leader works to generate behavioral change and link the change with accepted stakeholder strategic imperatives. Both of these steps act to minimize the controversial element of the change. The change leaders keep the focus on the strategic benefits of the change and attempt to keep the change from becoming a referendum between sets of deeply held values.

Branch Rickey and the Signing of Jackie Robinson

I illustrate this process using the example of a successful yet controversial organizational change: the actions leading to the racial integration of Major League Baseball in the United States. On April 15, 1947, the Brooklyn Dodgers opened the baseball season against the Boston Braves. Starting at first base was Jackie Robinson, the first black player to play in Major League Baseball (MLB) in the modern era. Over the next few years, Robinson would play a large part in transforming the Dodgers from lovable losers to envied winners. More importantly, he paved the way toward a broad desegregation of baseball. Jackie Robinson was the primary actor in the implementation of this change. However, the work of designing the change preceded Jackie Robinson's notable, historic leadership in making the change a success.

In fact, that day in April occurred years after the change effort had begun. Branch Rickey, the general manager and later part owner of the Brooklyn Dodgers, had been working toward Robinson's debut since 1943. I focus on the central role of Branch Rickey as the initiator and leader of this change initiative.

Desegregating baseball was a highly controversial action at the time. Segregated institutions were deeply ingrained in American culture, and few institutions were desegregated. Black Americans and white Americans operated in different social spheres. In the South, Jim Crow laws institutionalized racism, while in the North, deeply held norms limited racial interaction and encouraged social and professional segregation.

In 1942, Branch Rickey found himself wondering how he could make an impact "outside the park." He was in his early sixties and had a record as a successful, innovative executive. He became an avid reader of research about race relations and segregation and informed his friends and family that he intended to work toward the desegregation of Major League Baseball. In addition to being an astute businessman, Rickey was also a religious man, and throughout his life he struggled to align these two aspects of his value system. Racial segregation posed a unique opportunity to fuse these values. He began a series of exchanges with leading academic experts on the integration of institutions. Rickey viewed segregation as an issue with moral undertones, but he also saw a business opportunity to secure a deeper talent base for his base-ball team. The end result of these discussions was a deep under-standing that he could act in a manner that was simultaneously good for business and also good for the country.

In January 1943, Branch Rickey met with the Dodgers board of directors at the New York Athletic Club to get their approval. Rickey raised the issue of recruiting black ballplayers in the con-text of improving the depleted talent pool (World War II had reduced the quality of available players at the time). Rickey was given the okay to proceed, and he implored the board to keep the discussion secret in order for the Dodgers to keep ahead of other teams. By 1944, Rickey had the secret backing of the Dodgers board to recruit black ballplayers.

After fully investigating Jackie Robinson, Rickey decided that he was the best choice. He had a record of stellar athletic perfor-mance, experience playing on a desegregated sports team (as an All-American running back for the UCLA football team), and evi-dence that he was a man willing to take risks for something he believed in (his court martial in the army). On August 28, 1945, Rickey met with Robinson in Rickey's New York office. Robinson agreed to sign, and on October 23, 1945, Jackie Robinson signed a contract with the Montreal Royals, the Dodgers minor league club.

Breaking Out of Limited Mindsets: Reconceptualizing
What Is Possible with a New Local Mindset

Successful initiators of controversial change redefine that change into a less controversial change that is consistent with current social norms while at the same time prompting a rethinking of those norms. This reframing of the change enables the initiator to harness the current mental models of the influential stakeholders and redirect these models to accommodate the change. Branch

Rickey was able to fundamentally redefine the issues prior to his initiation of the change attempt. His redefinition enabled him to use numerous justifications for signing Jackie Robinson without betraying his belief in social justice.

Branch Rickey's actions were guided by two motives that initially seemed to be at odds with each other. The first motive was his insatiable drive to create a winning, profitable baseball team. The second motive was to live his life in a manner that was consistent with both his religious beliefs and his understanding of social justice. Rickey was able to reframe his world view such that these two motives were not only compatible but mutually reinforcing. In a sense he re-created his understanding of what was possible in his position in the Dodgers organization. By fusing these two motivating factors into a single justification for action, Rickey was able to plead his case in business vernacular without undermining his social justice motivations. Not once did Rickey make a statement that was at odds with his ideals of social justice. In fact, earlier letters indicated that Rickey felt that growing racial stress in America threatened to undermine the supports for a healthy capitalistic society.

Understanding Why Something Controversial Can Work: A Janusian Reframing

The first, and perhaps most significant, part of the controversial strategic change effort involves redefining the domain of possibility for social action. As mentioned earlier, controversial change challenges widely held norms. The first reaction many people have to such norm-challenging behavior is that the change is ill conceived because it is inconsistent with a realistic view of "how things work." Before the change initiators can sway the opinions of others, they must redefine their own understanding of how the social goal of their change effort (desegregation) can be complementary with other, more immediate goals of their organization (maintaining profitability). This reframing may require a type of paradoxical thinking. Rickey needed to understand how business and baseball success could be compatible with desegregation *before* he could convince others of its value.

For many years, researchers have associated paradoxical thinking with creativity, and Albert Rothenberg's concept of Janusian thinking is an example of this.[3] Janusian thinking enables the individual to hold two contradictory thoughts to be true simultaneously. The creative thinking triggered by Janusian thought leads to major insights and new world views. This type of thinking enables more flexibility in thought by freeing the individual from the preconceived notion that the opposites are incompatible. The resulting framework is often more than just a combining of the two antagonistic elements; it is a fusing of the two elements into a new framework that contains significant parts of each but also contains entirely new parts.

The tension-tracking exercise (chapter 9) could be the foundation of this type of reframing. Rather than trying to manage and understand the tensions, we try to fuse them into a fundamentally new understanding of the situation.

Sustainable Reframing: Fusing Divergent Ideas— Not Just Replacing One Idea with Another

E. F. Schumacher explains the implications of Janusian thinking in his discussion of convergent and divergent problems.[4] Convergent problems deal with distinct, precise, quantifiable, logical ideas that are amenable to empirical investigation. As these problems are studied in more depth, solutions tend to converge into a single accepted solution. Divergent problems are not easily quantifiable and do not have a single solution. As these problems are examined in more depth, the solutions diverge or become contradictory. Schumacher suggests that through the recognition of the divergent nature of a problem, we can generate a transformation as expectations of a right answer are relaxed.

Controversial strategic change is a divergent issue, and the breaking of social norms can have unpredictable results. However, the attempt to change the social structure of an organization does not by itself indicate paradoxical thinking. In order for the change to result in a transformation, the initiator must generate a new framework that challenges the status quo in a way that suggests the need for paradoxical thought. Social change attempts that do not fundamentally change the understanding of the issue will risk settling back to a modified status quo or fading away over time.

Rickey needed to not just show that desegregation was compatible with baseball success, but that desegregation was essential for future baseball success. Exercises that bring participants outside their comfort zone, such as blind-spot centering (chapter 3) and reverse default setting (chapter 11) can potentially trigger this type of frame transformation.

As another vivid example, consider the actions of Covington Hall, a poet and labor activist in the early twentieth century who attempted to mobilize Southern labor across racial lines. His approach was to appeal to the workers' gender identity rather than their racial identity.[5] He argued that union members were real men and questioned the masculinity of those workers who didn't organize to stand up to management. Initially, Hall's appeal was successful, but over time the racial division reemerged and divided the Southern labor movement.

One possible explanation for the short-lived success of this social change is that Hall's arguments show no evidence of paradoxical thought. He successfully shifted the frame of the discussion from race to a more inclusive (at least among union membership) gender framing, but he did not challenge, directly or indirectly, the underlying belief that black workers were inferior in some way to white workers. As a result, this division reemerged at a later time and was in some ways held more strongly because the belief had survived the labor upheaval.

From Insight to Action: Using the New Mindset
to Change Actions, Not Values

Developmental theory points out that individual value change cannot be forced from an external actor.[6] Such a transformation must come from an internal contradiction that can no longer be tolerated. A changing environment that exposes old mental models to new, potentially incompatible situations could be one way to create a value change. One way to trigger this transformation is to create a situation in which the individual must test his or her values through behavior. This is similar to the parenting technique of allowing a child to learn through experience rather than through a lecture. For example, the child's understanding of the need to bundle up in the winter may come less from parental pleas than from an experience of walking home with snow down his or her back and numb hands because mittens were left at home.

Changing Deeply Held Beliefs through Personal Experience

Controversial social change can be successfully accomplished by focusing on changing behaviors, not values. Once the behavior has been changed, the individual actors are able, and perhaps encouraged, to question their old value system. In effect, the change advocate creates the opportunity for a dialectic between the new organizational behaviors and the old organizational value system. One method for doing this is to downplay the social aspects of the change until after the behavioral change.

It was not until after Jackie Robinson was playing for the Brooklyn Dodgers that Rickey and Robinson began to speak about social justice as a motive for their actions. By that point, other people who were affected by the change had already begun to question their preconceived social value system. For example, Pee Wee Reese, who was not against signing Jackie Robinson but was skeptical at first, became a vocal advocate for desegregation over the next ten years. By not publicly pushing his social agenda, Rickey enabled the participants and observers to the Robinson signing to reconsider their beliefs about segregation by observing the success of both Robinson and the Dodgers. Such evidence is harder to dismiss, or to mobilize resources against, than abstract social justice arguments.

Rickey's initial linking of social justice with business strategy allowed him to anticipate the value change that could follow the behavioral change. He actively avoided social justifications while creating situations that challenged the social frameworks of the other individuals involved. Often, values are actively debated during social change attempts. The weakness of the current tradition system is brought into the open and actively debated. This is appropriate since social change is an attempt to change the dominant tradition system. The most direct way to do this is through directly challenging the offending tradition, yet Rickey avoided this values debate.

Baseball Desegregation as a Social Justice Issue

It is useful to contrast Branch Rickey's actions with those of William Benswanger. In 1944, Benswanger, president of the

Pittsburgh Pirates, made a public attempt to break baseball's color barrier. The Pirates invited two black players, Josh Gibson and Buck Leonard, to try out for the team. In a statement about the tryout, Benswanger said, "Colored men are American citizens with American rights...I know there are many problems connected with this question but after all, somebody has to make the first move." The tryout was well publicized and received a considerable amount of local and national attention. The public response, according to the Pirates, was overwhelming. The Pirates' office was flooded with protests and threats. As a result, Benswanger backed down and let the issue drop.

Benswanger justified his effort to integrate the Pirates as a matter of social justice and appealed to the common experience of World War II to make his case. The result was a strong negative reaction to the effort. Why? One possibility is that Benswanger's framing came into direct conflict with another more salient social belief: that of racial segregation and "separate but equal." By framing the discussion as a social issue, Benswanger invited others to respond to his actions using other social tradition arguments, namely, that "separate but equal" had worked or was an important cultural tradition.

Like Benswanger, Rickey viewed integration as a social issue right from the start. This is evident in his public reflections on the issue prior to 1945. However, unlike Benswanger, Rickey did not offer social justifications for his actions. From 1945 through 1947, Rickey explained his attempts to sign a black baseball player in business terms. To the team owners, he emphasized the strategic advantage of recruiting black players. To the players, he emphasized the increased chances of winning.

Not only did Rickey avoid talking about his actions in social terms, but he actively distanced his actions from those who attempted to attribute broad social motives to his actions. When it became clear that several journalists for black newspapers began to view him as their best hope to desegregate baseball, Rickey held a news conference to attack the integrity of the Negro league and announce the formation of his own Negro league team. This announcement had the effect of deflecting any public discussion of his ambitions to desegregate the Dodgers.

Linking Stakeholder Salience, Action, and Accepted Stakeholder Goals

The change agent must justify the change in such a manner that it addresses the concerns and needs of the various stakeholders. This involves careful analysis to identify the essential stakeholders and understand how the stakeholders view the organization's place in the broader society.

One immediately noticeable factor in Rickey's success was his in-depth knowledge of the concerns and goals of the various Dodgers stakeholders. The plan that Rickey developed in 1944, with the assistance of NYU sociologist Daniel Dodson, focused on winning the approval from multiple stakeholders *before* the player played for the Dodgers. Rickey used this knowledge to modify his arguments for the Robinson signing to appeal to the different stakeholders. He was able to do this without being insincere or manipulative because of his initial reframing of the situation.

As I noted earlier, Rickey's Janusian reformulation of the issue of desegregation enabled him to extol the strategic benefits of desegregation (for example, advantage over other teams, new potential fan base, higher-quality players) without betraying the social benefits. The limited vision that Rickey gave for the Robinson signing involved socially legitimate justifications, such as winning the World Series. Rickey's astute political actions combined his crucial insider knowledge of baseball with his newly developed, inclusive mental model of success.

Using Subtle Rather Than Bold Arguments
We often take as a given that a significant organizational change needs to be combined with a strong new organizational vision. The new vision articulates the organization's new perspective and place in its environment. During strategic change, such a vision is essential in order to coordinate and clarify the new organizational processes. The benefits of a forceful vision are not as clear during a process of *controversial* strategic change because controversial strategic change involves a rethinking of fundamental relationships within society. The participants actively question their traditions and values. Building a vision around a particular value structure can

alienate those groups or individuals who disagree with the value structure. An articulation of social vision may polarize the listeners into those who agree with the underlying values and those who don't. If the social vision advocates a minority view, then the vision articulation may have the effect of mobilizing powerful opposition to the social view. This countermobilization is likely to occur even when the proponents of the new social vision support their arguments with specific empirical evidence.

Rickey did not champion his actions as being a new direction for baseball and consistently downplayed the transformative nature of desegregation (at least initially). It was merely a new tactic for winning. It was hard to mobilize passionate opposition to the idea of making the Dodgers a better baseball team.

Using Accepted Topics and Structures to Make the Change an Insider Change

Rickey was a consummate insider and was well connected in the New York City media, political networks, and the business relationships of baseball. He knew, perhaps better than anyone else, which arguments would be persuasive with which people. He also knew how to wield his power and when to ease up and let someone else push the issue.

Executives, like everyone else, face the temptation to avoid controversial issues. A social change agent is faced with the daunting job of not only changing a particular organizational action but also changing the accepted rules of discourse in an organization. Many attempts at social change are sidetracked because the change is not considered a legitimate topic of conversation within the organization. One method for avoiding this pitfall is to use the current discourse patterns and content of the organization to justify the social change.[7] The social change can then be explained and sold to the various stakeholders in a way that appeals to the stakeholders' expectations of the organization.

It is difficult to mobilize people if the initiator is unable to link the change attempt with his or her immediate concerns. Branch Rickey was able to challenge the African-American leaders to support Robinson because he was able to tailor his justifications to match the concerns of the Brooklyn African-American community. In a similar way, Rickey communicated his plan to the players in a way that would resonate with them. These arguments could succeed because Rickey had a working understanding about which justifications for action were legitimate within the different stakeholder groups. Controversial change requires deep insider knowledge of the people, their positions, and the institutional norms.

Unquestioned Brilliance and Implementing Controversial Change

Once a leader makes a commitment to implement a change, the leader all too often rushes right into action. Prior to any public action, the change leader, with the assistance of a strong change team, should work through some key issues. The right questions can help a change team resist the call of comfortable yet limiting mindsets, while actively engaging with key stakeholders and confronting changing environments.

Questions to Guide Change Planning

Guiding definition

- What is the change? The change task needs to be clearly defined. If you are unable to clearly measure when the change has been successfully completed, then the task needs more definition. The process of defining the change includes identifying the "nonnegotiable" parts of the change.
- Who are the key stakeholders? There are numerous ways to classify stakeholders. One helpful exercise is to identify stakeholders who have the power to stop the change or an interest in the outcome of the change.
- Which stakeholders are likely to be most antagonistic toward the change?

Guiding strategic action

- What is the stakeholder engagement strategy? What is the order for approaching the stakeholders, and how will you approach them?

- What are the trigger points in the change process? A trigger point is something that has to happen in order for a change to be successful but that is outside the control of the change leader. Overconfidence can mask trigger points because we do not recognize them as outside our control.
- What are the underlying values that will frame the issue for the key stakeholders? This question should be addressed separately for each stakeholder.

Each one of these questions helps a change leader reframe the change in a manner that increases its odd for success. The answers to these questions start the process of reworking the change initiative to fit within the institutional and political environment. Taking the time to consider them at the beginning will save immense time and frustration during the implementation.

Implementing controversial strategic change in an organization is extremely difficult, and doing it well is particularly important. Controversial strategic change directly challenges widely accepted organizational norms, and, to be successful, it must change not only the members' behavior but also the members' interpretations of societal norms. Successfully initiating this type of an organizational change requires the creation of a new mental model that combines the seemingly incompatible social and strategic justifications for the change. Not content merely challenging conventional mindsets, the leader finds a way to create new local mindsets to facilitate the change.

Social change can be explained at various levels (individual, organizational, or societal), and the interpretation of actions will depend on how observers understand the reasons for the change. Interest groups will attempt to interpret actions in a manner that forwards their cause. A successful facilitator of controversial strategic change provides a justification for the change and actively distances the change from competing justifications.

Shining a Light on Brilliance  **13**

The Knowing-Doing Gap

Even if something seems obvious to us, we do not necessarily act upon that information. This was the theme of a book by Jeffrey Pfeffer and Robert Sutton called *The Knowing-Doing Gap*.[1] They make the point that the gap between knowing you should do something and actually doing it may be a more difficult gap to close for managers than the gap between knowledge and ignorance. Managers often know what they should do, but for various reasons, they do not do it.

The fundamental leadership trap at the core of this book absolutely falls into the category of tasks that may seem obvious to us, but which, for some reason, we do not act upon. The cycle of limited mindsets–confirmation bias–overconfidence, time pressure, fear of being wrong, and an unnoticed belief that we know more than those around us often get in our way.

I often view much of social science research as an exercise of restating something that someone else already observed many years ago. There is not much about human interaction that has not already been observed and recorded during the last 2,500 years. The well-designed social psychology study may simply find a way to empirically demonstrate a human tendency observed by long-dead philosophers. This does not mean that social science is useless; to the contrary, we need to be reminded. To be a social scientist is not to discover new knowledge as much as it is to translate old knowledge or to rediscover lost knowledge about the human condition.

It is fine to say that you already know that great leaders should seek alternative mindsets, learn to live with and seek patterns in uncertainties, seek helpers based on expertise, and modify plans as the environment changes around them. Each one of those statements sounds like common sense. And yet each one of us will also acknowledge that we rarely do these exercises in our own work, and we rarely observe our leaders doing these things. We all need to do a better job bridging the knowing-doing gap.

The techniques in this book provide some ideas about how you can start bridging this gap. The techniques are not complex. In fact, the risk with these techniques is that they are deceptively simple. By trying to keep them simple and easy to recall, I run the risk of making them feel too obvious. In my mind, obvious is good. Obvious makes it more likely that you will remember at least part of one technique the next time you find yourself needing to broaden the mindsets of your team. Donald Sull and Kathleen Eisenhardt make a wonderful case that simple rules may be just what is required to succeed in a complex world in their book *Simple Rules*.[2] The unquestioned brilliance techniques are a way to keep yourself honest about what you know while also giving you needed guidance for managing uncertainty.

Drop Your Tools

In his well-known 1996 article, organizational theorist Karl Weick retells the story of the deaths of twenty-seven wild-land firefighters in two separate firefighting disasters. He observes that many of these firemen lost their lives within a short distance of safety, and many were still carrying their heavy equipment when they died. He asked the question: why did they not drop their tools so that they could move faster?[3] Weick's examination of this question has application for challenging our unquestioned brilliance.

Why we don't drop our tools:

- Control—Tools give us control over the environment. Once we drop our tools, we admit we are in uncharted territory.
- Skill at dropping—We don't know how to drop them. We spend lots of time teaching people when to use their tools, but we don't spend much time teaching people when it is time to discard them.
- Skill with replacement activity—We spend years applying certain tools. We may be aware of alternative tools (in the case of the firefighters, these would be escaping fires and fire shelters), but we have little experience using them.
- Failure—Holding tools postpones admission of failure. As long as you hold onto a tool to fight a fire, there is hope you can put the fire out. Once you discard it, you are admitting that your goal has changed because you did not meet your initial goal.
- Social dynamics—Looking at your leader, the danger is behind you. The firefighters were moving up a steep slope and focused on the person in front of them. The fire was behind them, and it was the person at the back of the line who most understood the urgency of the situation. The focus on the leader can be healthy only if the leader truly understands the situation at hand.
- Consequences—Believe it won't make a difference. Dropping tools is a risky act. We will do it only if we feel it will give us a real chance to succeed that we would not have otherwise.
- Identity—We are our tools. Our professional identity is tied up in our tools: firefighters with their shovels and chainsaws, police officers with their weapons, financial analysts with their valuation models, software programmers with their computers, salespeople with their customer databases—you get the idea. It can be terrifying to set these aside. Our tools give us our credibility. It is who we are.

Weick's analogy is apt for our task of challenging unquestioned brilliance. The routines that got you here may be the very routines that now get in your way. If your skills (your tools) were developed to help you succeed in a different world or in a different job, it may be time to start experimenting with some new tools. You do not forget all that you have learned through your experience. Rather, you learn to use your experience in a new way. Our goal is not to replace unquestioned brilliance with uncertain ignorance but to ground our brilliance in reality rather than in delusion.

The analogy offered by Weick is an appropriate reminder that it is not easy to break out of tried-and-true routines. There is a reason we have those habits: they have worked more often than not in our past. How confident are you that the future will conform to *your* past?

Commitment to Truth

One of the interesting things about writing a book about leadership is the realization that the people most likely to buy and read a book about improving leadership are those who are already darned good leaders. Those who most need to improve are those least likely to seek improvement. For this reason, I feel comfortable making a blanket statement about anyone who is still reading this book. You are already a good leader. I hope this book has given you one or two ideas of how to become a better leader.

Personal mastery is one of the five disciplines for creating learning organizations described by Peter Senge in his seminal book *The Fifth Discipline*.[4] Personal mastery requires a personal vision, creative tension, and a commitment to the truth. The ten techniques in this book certainly can contribute to all three, but at the end of the day, commitment to the truth requires effort on your part, regardless of techniques used.

Senge describes commitment to the truth as including a willingness to uncover ways we limit and deceive ourselves and a willingness to challenge the way things are. Such a commitment leads to a deepening awareness of structures that underlie and generate events. Such awareness leads to the ability to change the structure to produce the results you seek.

My challenge to you is to go back over the chapters of this book and pick one technique that resonates with you and fits your role. Make a commitment to use it. Once you try the technique, modify it to make it work even better! Sometimes it is the simple discussion that triggers the insight. Some real examples I've seen include the following:

- A key account manager combined blind-spot centering with stakeholder mapping to redesign his sales calls and increased his contract size and success rate.
- The management team of a construction materials company used uncertainty vectoring and the HERE snapshot to identify new potential partners outside the traditional construction industry.
- A chief information officer started using the TAP Check when assigning tasks and found increased morale and project quality in the project teams.

Each of these leaders picked just one or two techniques to use, but each of them also found a way to make those techniques drive insight and action. I'd call that brilliance.

Appendix: Technique Instructions

For easy reference, here are the steps for each of the techniques described in this book. GSO decision making (chapter 7) is not included because it is a diagnostic rule of thumb rather than a technique with specific steps. This is a bare-bones description of the techniques. See the corresponding chapter for more details.

Blind-Spot Centering (Chapter 3)
Step 1: Generate a list of shared assumptions.
Each person identifies three assumptions that are widely shared within the organization, one shared assumption about customers or potential customers, one shared assumption about competitors (or other relevant organizations if competition is not relevant to your organization), and one shared assumption about the organization. Combine the individual responses into a single list sorted by customer, competitor, and organization.

Step 2: Select dominant assumptions.
Divide into three subgroups. Assign each subgroup to focus on customer, competitor, or organization assumptions. Each subgroup decides which assumption on their list is the most deeply or widely held assumption within the organization.

Step 3: Assume reversal/blind-spot centering.
Each subgroup is to imagine the widely held assumption selected in step 2 is incorrect. They will then generate an alternate assumption.

Step 4: Describe the world.
If the assumption identified in step 3 were true, what would the environment look like? List some assumptions about this imaginary world. How would customers be different? Suppliers? Competitors? Employees? Are there any assumptions listed in step 1 that would still hold true? If so, list these as well.

Step 5: Create a combined map of assumptions.
Combine the work of the three groups onto a single Venn diagram. Make note of the overlapping assumptions. Groups should also add assumptions from the other groups to their lists, if they fit, and move them to the overlapping area of the Venn diagram.

Step 6: Compare assumptions to the original list.
Compare the blind-spot centered Venn diagram to the original list of assumptions made in step 1. Highlight any assumptions that remain on both lists.

Uncertainty Vectoring (Chapter 4)
Step 1: Define the destination.
We need to define our focus before we can do any useful work with uncertainties. The focus needs to include the area of interest and time horizon. For our example, the area of interest is the bar industry in an American college town, and the time horizon is five years in the future.

Step 2: Identify key uncertainties: The PEST+ brainstorming structure.

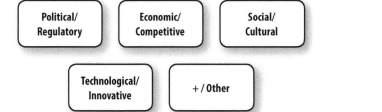

Step 3: Identify the ten highest-impact uncertainties.

Step 4: Identify the current state on the uncertainty continuum.
For each uncertainty, define the end points of the range and place an X on the point in that range that represents the current state.

Step 5: Create the uncertainty vector chart.

The Backward-Forward Flip (Chapter 5)

Step 1: Identify a surprise event from the industry past.
Identify two to three industry surprises defined as events, shifts, or innovations that were not predicted, or even expected at all, by conventional industry wisdom.

Step 2: List justifications for conventional wisdom—past.
List all the reasons industry experts gave at the time to explain why this event would not happen.

Step 3: Ask why conventional wisdom was wrong—past.
List all the reasons industry experts were wrong in their assessment. What had conventional wisdom missed?

Step 4: Identify a current potential industry shift.
Identify a high-impact industry shift that a majority of industry experts currently do not expect to occur.

Step 5: Consider why this shift will not occur.
Step 5 mirrors step 2 except that we are now considering the question as it relates to the current, potential industry shift.

Step 6: Consider why this shift will occur.
List the changes in the world that would enable and potentially trigger the industry shift to occur.

Step 7: Rank the probability of items identified in step 6.
Sort the list created in step 6 from most to least likely to occur. Starting with the most likely to occur and moving to the least likely item on the list, discuss the most likely scenario that could lead to this industry shift.

TAP Check (Chapter 6)

Step 1: Clearly define the team's task. Include any subtasks or execution requirements in the task definition.

Step 2: Generate a list of abilities that are either (1) required in order for the team to compete the task, or (2) desired in order for the team to more effectively complete the task. Sort each ability on the list into either the required or the desired category.

3: Identify specific people who possess the abilities. It is acceptable to name a person multiple times if he or she possesses more than one of the listed abilities.

Step 4: If you are also interested in developing team member abilities, create a second list of team members who need or want to develop the identified abilities.

TAP Team Expertise Assessment (Chapter 6)

Step 1: Identify the top ten abilities required for team success.

Step 2: Create the assessment instrument.
Team members will be asked to assess four aspects for each ability:

1. Rate the overall expertise level of the team.
2. Rate the range of ability on the team. Is the expertise of the most skilled person on the team far greater than the expertise of the least skilled person on the team?

3. Identify the person on the team with the most expertise or skill for the ability.
4. Rate your own expertise.

Step 3: Administer the survey and collect the results.

Step 4: Score the team.

Step 5: Have a team conversation about the assessment results.

Stakeholder Mapping (Chapter 8)
Step 1: Draw the power and interest grid on a flip chart (refer to Figure 8-1).

Figure 8-1

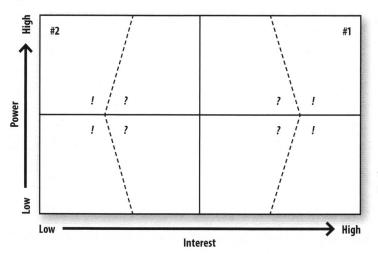

Step 2: Start by identifying high-power/high-interest stakeholders.

Step 3: Shift over to the left side of the grid and try to identify high-power/low-interest stakeholders.

Step 4: Identify stakeholder salience.

Step 5: Map stakeholders based on the three salience attributes.

Tension Tracking (Chapter 9)

Step 1: Identify key tensions.

Generate a list of tensions that pull your focus in opposite directions or that operate as competing interests when you are forced to make decisions. Start by thinking about decisions you make on a daily or weekly basis. When you cannot think of more tensions, shift your time horizon to a monthly or quarterly basis. After this, shift to a yearly basis and, finally, to a five- to seven-year basis.

Step 2: Identify roles connected with one side of the tension.

Pick one or two tensions that consistently generate the most stress as you work to accomplish your objectives. Identify the roles within your organization (or with external partners, if applicable to your work) whose interests most closely align with one side of the chosen tension.

Step 3: List benefits of both sides of the tension.

Take the perspective of each of the roles identified in step 2 and list the benefits that are derived from taking that perspective.

Step 4: Connect actions with benefits on both sides of the tension.

Examine your list of benefits from step 3 and make reasonable, realistic connections between the action you hope to sustain and some of those benefits.

The HERE Snapshot (Chapter 10)

Helpers

> The key question: Whom do you need to know?
> Conduct a stakeholder mapping exercise.

End Game

> The key question: What does success look like *here*?
> Describe the day in the future when you arrive at work and it is clear the initiative has been completely successful.

Reconnaissance

> The key question: What can't you know?
> Conduct a PEST+ exercise.

Errors

The key question: Where are you wrong?

HERE Questions and Tasks
1. Pivot Points

   1a. Identify key pivot points in your plan. Pivot points
       are those moments that will determine if your
       initiative jumps over to a path leading to failure or
       continues on a path toward a successful outcome.
   1b. For each pivot point, identify the early warning signs
       that may indicate the initiative is off track.
   1c. Identify one or two mitigating actions the team can
       take to keep the initiative on track.
   1d. Assign ownership of monitoring this to individual
       members of the implementation team.
2. Core Assumptions
   2a. Which of the uncertainties listed in the reconnais-
       sance step are most uncertain? In other words, which
       are the hardest to predict with certainty?
   2b. How will this uncertainty affect the initiative?
   2c. How are you monitoring this uncertainty?
   2d. Assign ownership of monitoring this to individual
       members of the implementation team.
3. Key Participants
   3a. Which key stakeholders do you know the least
       about? What role will those stakeholders play in
       implementing this initiative?
   3b. What would you wish to know about them?
   3c. How will you get that information?
   3d. Assign ownership of engaging with these stakeholders
       to individual members of the implementation team.

Reverse Default Setting (Chapter 11)
Step 1: Define your default setting.

Step 2: Reverse your default.
What if your default-assumed outcome turns out not to be true?
How would outcomes be different? Would different stakeholders

be involved? What are some reasonable trigger events that could shift reality into this nondefault future?

Step 3: Design a question to test your default assumption.
What question can you ask that will help you test your assumption, and whom will you ask?

Step 4: Identify early warning signs.
What are the early warning signs that the world may not be moving toward the default-predicted outcome? How will you track those signs? How often will you check them?

Notes

1. Charles G. Lord, Lee Ross, and Mark R. Lepper, "Biased Assimilation and Attitude Polarization: The Effects of Prior Theories on Subsequently Considered Evidence," *Journal of Personality and Social Psychology* 37, no. 11 (1979): 2098–109.

2. In actuality, we may seek less disconfirming evidence in those situations in which we are less confident of our position. When asked to make a guess about something we cannot possibly know, we have more reason to suspect we may be wrong and feel a greater need to build an argument in support of the initial guess. See Dolores Albarracín and Amy L. Mitchell, "The Role of Defensive Confidence in Preference for Proattitudinal Information: How Believing That One Is Strong Can Sometimes Be a Defensive Weakness," *Personality and Social Psychology Bulletin* 30, no. 12 (2004): 1565–84.

3. Learning about quantum physics is one of my many well-developed techniques for procrastination. Some people play Candy Crush; I learn about random academic fields. I suspect both approaches offer their share of distraction and frustration.

4. British cartoonist William Ely Hill printed "My Wife and My Mother-in-Law" in *Puck*, an American humor magazine, in the November 1915 issue, with the caption, "They are both in this picture—Find them" (11). The figure has a strong resemblance to other images that circulated on anonymous postcards and advertisements as far back as 1888. It is widely assumed that Hill adapted his image from those. According to Jack Botwinick, the figure was introduced to the profession of psychology in an article by Edwin Boring in 1930. See "Husband and Father-in-Law—A Reversible Figure," *American Journal of Psychology* 74, no. 2 (1961): 312–13.

5. *Eureka* derives from the ancient Greek word *heúrēka*, which has been roughly translated as, "I have found it." The use of the term to describe a sudden flash of brilliance is popularly attributed to Archimedes in a story about him initially written by Vitruvius two hundred years after Archimedes lived. Many historians and scientists doubt that the story is based on reality, but the phrase lives on because of its ability to express the

sense of joy in discovery. An editor once told me not to use the term *eureka moment* because the reference was too "American." We can thank the American gold rush for this misconception. The term is Greek, not American.

6. Melanie Rudd, Kathleen Vohs, and Jennifer Aaker, "Awe Expands People's Perception of Time, Alters Decision Making, and Enhances Well-Being," *Psychological Science* 23, no. 10 (2012): 1130–36.

7. John R. Austin, "Measuring Cross-Functional Team Expertise at Outdoor Living Company," in *Organizational Behavior: A Management Challenge*, ed. Linda K. Stroh, Gregory B. Northcraft, and Margaret A. Neale (Mahwah, NJ: Erlbaum, 2002), 169.

8. John Beard and Rebecca Stoltzfus, "Iron Deficiency Anemia: Reexamining the Nature and Magnitude of the Public Health Problem, Proceedings of a Conference, May 21–24, 2000, Belmont, Maryland, USA," supplement, *Journal of Nutrition* 131, no. 2S-2 (2001): 563S–703S.

9. Eleanor Smith, "The Good-Luck Charm That Solved a Public Health Problem," *Atlantic*, January–February 2014.

10. Margaret Rhodes, "This Iron Fish Offers Relief from Anemia," *Fast Company*, July 26, 2013. For more on the Lucky Iron Fish project, go to www.luckyironfish.com.

11. My approach to reframing is based on William Gamson's work on reframing in social movements: *Strategy of Social Protest* (Belmont, CA: Wadsworth, 1975). I had the pleasure of taking a course with Professor Gamson in graduate school. His writing influenced the design and research questions we asked in our project on corporate activism of LGBT activists: W. E. Douglas Creed, Maureen A. Scully, and John R. Austin, "Clothes Make the Person? The Tailoring of Legitimating Accounts and the Social Construction of Identity," *Organization Science* 13, no. 5 (2002): 475–96. For a good description of the process as used in organizations, see W. E. Douglas Creed, Jeffrey A. Langstraat, and Maureen A. Scully, "A Picture of the Frame: Frame Analysis as Technique and as Politics," *Organizational Research Methods* 5, no. 1 (2002): 34–55.

12. For a thorough overview of theoretical and empirical research on confirmation bias, see Raymond S. Nickerson, "Confirmation Bias: A Ubiquitous Phenomenon in Many Guises," *Review of General Psychology* 2, no. 2 (1998): 175.

13. Daniel Kahneman and Dan Lovallo, "Timid Choices and Bold Forecasts: A Cognitive Perspective on Risk Taking," *Management Science* 39, no. 1 (1993): 17–31.

14. Hal Arkes and Peter Ayton, "Call It Quits," *New Scientist* 158, no. 2135 (1998): 40–43.

15. Eta S. Berner and Mark L. Graber, "Overconfidence as a Cause of Diagnostic Error in Medicine," *American Journal of Medicine* 121, no. 5 (2008): S2–S23.

16. Susan Joslyn and Jared LeClerc, "The 'Cry Wolf' Effect and Weather-Related Decision Making," Decision Making with Uncertainty, University of Washington, May 9, 2013, depts.washington.edu/forecast/wordpress/wp-content/uploads/2013/06/NDM-poster_5.9.13.pdf.

17. Interestingly, there is some research suggesting that we prefer to have uncertainty included in our weather forecasts. See Rebecca E. Morss,

Julie L. Demuth, and Jeffrey K. Lazo, "Communicating Uncertainty in Weather Forecasts: A Survey of the US Public," *Weather and Forecasting* 23, no. 5 (2008): 974–91.

18. For a good overview of overconfidence research, see Daniel Kahneman, *Thinking, Fast and Slow* (New York: Farrar, Straus and Giroux, 2011), pt. 3, chaps. 19–24.

19. I was always tempted in these situations to reply, "Apparently, not anymore," but managed to resist that urge.

20. In an excellent two-decade-long study, Philip E. Tetlock demonstrated that the accuracy of political pundits was no better than chance. Those pundits with a particularly strong ideological position fared even worse, as would be predicted by the confirmation bias. *Expert Political Judgment: How Good Is It? How Can We Know?* (Princeton: Princeton University Press, 2005), 125–28. In the television pundits' defense, their job is to give simple answers that are simultaneously pithy and provocative. I suppose it is unfair to criticize them for simply doing their job well, but it is a role that illustrates the "not knowing what we don't know" trap quite clearly.

21. See, for example, Neal J. Roese and Kathleen D. Vohs, "Hindsight Bias," *Perspectives on Psychological Science* 7, no. 5 (2012): 411–26. A seminal article on this topic is Baruch Fischhoff and Ruth Beyth, "'I Knew It Would Happen': Remembered Probabilities of Once-Future Things," *Organizational Behaviour and Human Performance* 13, no. 1 (1975): 1–16.

22. Discussions periodically pop up regarding the value of going to a highly competitive, elite university versus a less prestigious university. These discussions are excellent examples of the role of issue framing in public debates. There are persuasive arguments to be made for and against attending a prestigious university. Unfortunately, those individuals making the case for one side or the other are often blind to the alternate frame being used by their antagonists. As a point of disclosure, I attended Johns Hopkins University as an undergraduate, but I do not own that shirt . . . yet.

23. Martin E. P. Seligman, *Authentic Happiness: Using the New Positive Psychology to Realize Your Potential for Lasting Fulfillment* (New York: Free Press/Simon and Schuster, 2002).

Chapter 2

1. I first outlined the three translation challenges in John R. Austin, "Making knowledge actionable: Three key translation moments," *Journal of Organization Design* 2, no. 3 (2013): 29-37. This chapter builds from that article.

2. Clifford Geertz, *Local Knowledge: Further Essays in Interpretive Anthropology* (New York: Basic Books, 1983).

3. See John R. Austin and Jean M. Bartunek, "Theories and Practices of Organization Development," in *The Handbook of Psychology: Vol. 12, Industrial and Organizational Psychology*, ed. Walter C. Borman, Daniel R. Ilgen, and Richard J. Klimoski (New York: Wiley, 2003), 309-32. We make the case that barriers to translation explain why there is such a strong divide between academics and practitioners in the field of organizational change.

4. Barbara Czarniawska and Bernward Joerges, "Travels of Ideas," in *Translating Organizational Change*, ed. Barbara Czarniawska and Guje Sevón (New York: De Gruyter, 1996), 13–48.

5. Richard J. Bernstein, *Praxis and Action: Contemporary Philosophies of Human Activity* (Philadelphia: University of Pennsylvania Press, 1971).

6. J. Stephen Lansing, *Priests and Programmers: Technologies of Power in the Engineered Landscape of Bali* (Princeton: Princeton University Press, 1991).

7. John R. Austin, "A Method for Facilitating Controversial Social Change in Organizations: Branch Rickey and the Brooklyn Dodgers," *Journal of Applied Behavioral Science* 33, no 1 (1997): 101–18.

8. Jack B. Soll and Richard P. Larrick, "Strategies for Revising Judgment: How (and How Well) People Use Others' Opinions," *Journal of Experimental Psychology: Learning, Memory, and Cognition* 35, no. 3 (2009): 780–805.

9. This story is also included in John R. Austin, *Leading Effective Change: A Primer for the HR Professional* (Alexandria, VA: SHRM Foundation, 2015).

10. Donald N. Sull with Yong Wang, "Outcycle the Competition: How Chinese Entrepreneurs Compete in Unpredictable Markets," chap. 4 in *Made in China: What Western Managers Can Learn from Trailblazing Chinese Entrepreneurs* (Boston: Harvard Business School Press, 2008).

Part II

1. As a principal at Decision Strategies International, I facilitated hundreds of groups through the scenario planning technique described in Paul J. H. Schoemaker and Robert E. Gunther, *Profiting from Uncertainty: Strategies for Succeeding No Matter What the Future Brings* (New York: London: Free Press, 2002). Decision Strategies International was founded by Dr. Schoemaker. Blue ocean strategy focuses on innovation and reconceptualizing competition and offers a number of useful techniques for challenging dominant frames. W. Chan Kim and Renée Mauborgne, *Blue Ocean Strategy: How to Create Uncontested Market Space and Make the Competition Irrelevant* (Boston: Harvard Business School Press, 2005).

2. Daniel Kahneman and Amos Tversky, "Choices, Values, and Frames," *American Psychologist* 39, no. 4 (1984): 341.

3. Varda Liberman, Steven M. Samuels, and Lee Ross, "The Name of the Game: Predictive Power of Reputations Versus Situational Labels in Determining Prisoner's Dilemma Game Moves," *Personality and Social Psychology Bulletin* 30, no. 9 (2004): 1175–85.

Chapter 3

1. David Foster Wallace, "This Is Water: Some Thoughts, Delivered on a Significant Occasion, about Living a Compassionate Life, Little, Brown, and Company" (transcript of the commencement speech given by David Foster Wallace at Kenyon College on May 21, 2005).

2. John A. Bargh, "Attention and Automaticity in Processing of Self-Relevant Information," *Journal of Personality and Social Psychology*, 43 (1982): 425–36.

3. Arthur C. Graesser, Stanley B. Woll, Daniel J. Kowalski, and Donald A. Smith, "Memory for Typical and Atypical Actions in Scripted Activities," *Journal of Experimental Psychology: Human Learning and Memory* 6 (1980): 503–15.

4. Ellen J. Langer, "Minding Matters: The Consequences of Mindlessness-Mindfulness," *Advances in Experimental Social Psychology* 22 (1989): 137–73.

5. John R. Austin and Jean M. Bartunek, "Theories and Practices of Organization Development," in *The Handbook of Psychology: Vol. 12. Industrial and Organizational Psychology*, ed. Walter C. Borman, Daniel R. Ilgen, and Richard J. Klimoski (New York: Wiley, 2003), 309–32.

6. Max H. Bazerman and Dolly Chugh, "Bounded Awareness: Focusing Failures in Negotiation," in *Negotiation Theory and Research: Frontiers of Social Psychology*, ed. Leigh L. Thompson (New York: Taylor & Francis Group, 2006).

7. Barry M. Staw, Lance E. Sandelands, and Jane E. Dutton. "Threat Rigidity Effects in Organizational Behavior: A Multilevel Analysis." *Administrative Science Quarterly* (1981): 501–24.

8. Meryl Reis Louis and Robert I. Sutton, "Switching Cognitive Gears: From Habits of Mind to Active Thinking," *Human Relations* 44 (1991): 55–76.

9. For a more in-depth discussion of cognitive modes and their relationship to group diversity, creativity, and conflict, see John R. Austin, "A Cognitive Framework for Understanding Demographic Influences in Groups," *The International Journal of Organizational Analysis* 5 (no. 4, 1997): 342–59. Incidentally, this was the very first article I wrote as a graduate student. Reading it approximately twenty years later, I am struck by how enduring this conceptual frame has been in my work. As in any model, it has blind spots, yet it continues to provide clarity and focus for how we lead groups. While I regret that I did not attempt to publish this article in a more visible outlet, I am heartened by how much this way of viewing creativity and conflict in teams has influenced subsequent approaches to understanding how team diversity affects team outcomes.

10. Thomas Mussweiler, Fritz Strack, and Tim Pfeiffer, "Overcoming the Inevitable Anchoring Effect: Considering the Opposite Compensates for Selective Accessibility," *Personality and Social Psychology Bulletin* 26 (2000): 1142–50.

11. I recognize that delivering bags to a gate ramp is a more time-consuming process, but try not to let that glaring fact get in the way of a good story

Chapter 4

1. The most famous of these was a study by Baruch Fischhoff and Ruth Beyth in which they asked people to predict what President Nixon would do in foreign policy. After the president famously, and to many unexpectedly, engaged with China and Russia, we asked participants what events they had said would happen on their earlier surveys. People consistently overestimated their predictions of events that ended up occurring.

Other studies have found similar results around subsequent public events. Baruch Fischhoff, and Ruth Beyth, "I Knew It Would Happen: Remembered Probabilities of Once Future Things," *Organizational Behavior and Human Performance* 13 (1975): 1–16.

2. Jonathan Baron and John C. Hershey, "Outcome Bias in Decision Evaluation," *Journal of Personality and Social Psychology* 54 (1988): 569–79.

3. Jon Birger, "EOG's Big Gamble on Shale Oil," *Fortune*, August 15, 2011.

4. Incidentally, I've found this attitude exists in most industries. Part of what is fascinating to me, as someone who works across multiple industries, is that most industries are nowhere near as complex as industry insiders like to believe. Once you work your way through the acronyms and industry-speak, which play a role in helping industry experts demonstrate insider status and identify outsiders, you find a shared set of strategic industry challenges.

5. Leigh Thompson, Dedra Gentner, and Jeffrey Loewenstein, "Avoiding Missed Opportunities in Managerial Life: Analogical Training More Powerful Than Individual Case Training," *Organizational Behavior & Human Decision Processes* 82, no. 1 (2000): 60–75; and Simone Moran, Yoella Bereby-Meyer, and Max Bazerman, "Stretching the Effectiveness of Analogical Training in Negotiations: Learning Core Principles for Creating Value," *Negotiation & Conflict Management Research* 1, no. 2 (2008): 99–134.

6. Francis J. Aguilar, *Scanning the Business Environment* (New York: Macmillan, 1967).

7. George Day and Paul Schoemaker have written a series of excellent articles on monitoring the environment. My favorite is George S. Day and Paul J. H. Schoemaker, "Scanning the Periphery," *Harvard Business Review* (November 2005): 135–48.

8. Paul J. H. Schoemaker, "Scenario Planning: A Tool for Strategic Thinking," *Sloan Management Review* 37, no. 2 (1995): 25–40. As a point of disclosure, I've worked with Decision Strategies International since 2008. This company was founded by Paul Schoemaker.

9. Scenario building as a planning tool has been in use since the 1960s. Initially it was used in the public policy planning field. Scenario planning was adopted for long-term planning purposes in the late 1960s/early 1970s by several global companies, most notably Exxon and Shell oil companies. The Shell process is the one that has had the most influence on scenario building techniques, primarily because several of the designers of the Shell technique left the company and became consultants. Some other great resources for understanding the building of scenarios and use of the outcomes are Kees van der Heijden, *Scenarios: The Art of Strategic Conversation*, 2nd ed. (New York: John Wiley & Sons, 2005); and Peter Schwartz, *The Art of the Long View: Planning for the Future in an Uncertain World* (New York: Doubleday, 1996).

Chapter 5

1. See Aaron Bobrow-Strain's book *White Bread: A Social History of the Store-Bought Loaf* (Boston: Beacon Press, 2013) for more on the history of mass-produced bread.

2. Carmen Reinhart and Kenneth Rogoff, *This Time Is Different: Eight Centuries of Financial Folly* (Princeton, NJ: Princeton University Press, 2009).

3. Walmart was extolled for their skill at managing their supply-chain, scale, and phenomenal growth. The story is quite different if we were to examine their approaches to employee relations.

4. Paul Slovic and Baruch Fischhoff, "On the Psychology of Experimental Surprises," *Journal of Experimental Psychology: Human Perception and Performance* 3, no. 4 (1977): 544–51.

5. Michael Bar-Eli, Ofer H. Azar, Ilana Ritov, Yael Keidar-Levin, and Galit Schein, "Action Bias among Elite Soccer Goalkeepers: The Case of Penalty Kicks," *Journal of Economic Psychology* 28, no. 5 (2007): 606–21.

6. Marion Fourcade, Etienne Ollion, and Yann Algan, "The Superiority of Economists," *Journal of Economic Perspectives* 29, no. 1 (2015): 89–114.

Part III

1. Two excellent books for further developing the strategic thinking capabilities of your team are Rob-Yan de Jong, *Anticipate: The Art of Leading by Looking Ahead* (New York: AMACOM, 2015); and Steven Krupp and Paul J. H. Schoemaker, *Winning the Long Game: How Strategic Leaders Shape the Future* (New York: Public Affairs, 2014).

Chapter 6

1. John R. Austin, "Expertise and Friendship: Help Seeking Efficacy in Groups," *Academy of Management Best Paper Proceedings* (2003).

2. Yuqing Ren and Linda Argote, "Transactive Memory Systems, 1985–2010: An Integrative Framework of Key Dimensions, Antecedents, and Consequences," *Academy of Management Annals* 5, no. 1 (2011): 189–229.

3. John R. Austin, "Transactive Memory in Organizational Groups: The Effects of Content, Consensus, Specialization, and Accuracy on Group Performance," *Journal of Applied Psychology* 88, no. 5 (2003): 866–78.

4. David P. Brandon and Andrea B. Hollingshead, "Transactive Memory Systems in Organizations: Matching Tasks, Expertise and People," *Organization Science* 15, no. 6 (2004): 633–44.

5. Daniel M. Wegner, "Transactive Memory: A Contemporary Analysis of the Group Mind," in *Theories of Group Behavior*, ed. Brian Mullen and George R. Goethals (New York: Springer- Verlag, 1987), 185–208.

6. Austin, "Transactive Memory," 866–878.

7. Brandon and Hollingshead, "Transactive Memory Systems," 633–44.

8. The TEP framework is essentially an associative network of task-related expertise. Associative network models describe mental models as consisting of numerous nodes (cognitive elements such as memories or pieces of knowledge) that are linked together to create a coherent picture. Over time, certain nodes develop strong links with each other if they are frequently called into working memory together. As a result, if one node is called into working memory, the second node may be automatically called into working memory. Nodes with multiple strong links are likely to be

called into working memory more frequently. The nodes that are called into working memory in a given situation will lead to a cognitive representation unique to that situation but related to previous similar situations. A person with multiple experiences in similar situations will have a well-developed set of nodes closely linked together that can be activated. A person with less expertise in such a situation may rely on a set of weaker links to attempt to make sense of the situation. During sense making, individuals will access associative networks with numerous links to the situation first. Subsequent associative networks will be accessed only to the extent that the initial associative network is deemed insufficient for solving the problem at hand. Thus, associative networks are nested within each other. The primary associative network is determined based on the quantity of its links to the problem at hand. A well-developed TEP unit is similar to a high-quality associative network and is more likely to be accessed in an appropriate situation. If this endnote did not scare you away and you want to read more, see John R. Austin and Ralph Hanke, "The Emerging Story of Transactive Memory in Teams: A Review and Synthesis of Transactive Memory Research" (paper presented at the Academy of Management Meetings, Honolulu, 2005).

9. This approach is consistent with theories that propose that activated social representations combine elements of context-specific exemplars with more generalized schematic representations. See Jeffery W. Sherman, "Development and Mental Representation of Stereotypes," *Journal of Personality and Social Psychology* 70 (1996): 1126–41.

10. Ciaran Heavey and Zeki Simsek, "Transactive Memory Systems and Firm Performance: An Upper Echelons Perspective," *Organization Science*. Published online in *Articles in Advance,* May 6, 2015:1–19.

Chapter 7

1. Yes, I know "decide" does not rhyme with the other three. I am relieved by that fact. The incessant rhyming in the field of team training is a pet peeve of mine. I always felt more than a little embarrassed teaching the Bruce Tuckman team development model to MBA students (forming, storming, norming, performing). The model is actually quite valuable as a guide, but it is hard to escape the kindergarten-like feel of rhyming models. As it is, many MBA students do not see a need to take team leadership seriously as a skill. Rhyming models don't help! In 1977, Tuckman and Jensen added a fifth stage to the model: adjourning. Seriously? First, it does not really rhyme. Second, seriously? Do we think teams will forget to stop working if we don't include that stage in a developmental framework? See Bruce W. Tuckman, "Developmental Sequence in Small Groups," *Psychological Bulletin* 63 (1965): 384–399; and Bruce W. Tuckman and Mary Ann C. Jensen, "Stages in Small Group Development Revisited," *Group and Organizational Studies* 2 (1977): 419–27. To Professor Tuckman and his students: The stage model is great, really! Well, other than that whole adjourning thing—I just can't quite see the point of that. I recall the four-stage model helped many of the students in my facilitation course successfully diagnose

team dysfunctions. The rhyming issue says more about me than about your model. So, we're cool, right?

2. Robert W. Keidel, "Baseball, Football, and Basketball: Models for Business," *Organizational Dynamics* 12, no. 3 (1985): 5–18. See Robert Keidel, "Team Sports Metaphors in Perspective," *Organizational Dynamics* 43 (December 2014): 294–302 for an excellent, updated global take on using team metaphors to examine organizations. James D. Thompson, *Organizations in Action: Social Science Bases of Administrative Theory*. Vol. 1 (Piscataway, NJ: Transaction Publishers, 2011).

3. For a great discussion of using sports teams as models for workplace teams, see Nancy Katz, "Sports Teams as a Model for Workplace Teams: Lessons and Liabilities," *Academy of Management Executive* 15, no. 3 (2001): 56–67.

4. Mihaly Csikszentmihalyi, *Flow: The Psychology of Optimal Experience* (New York: Harper & Row, 1990). Jeanne Nakamura and Mihaly Csikszentmihalyi, "Flow Theory and Research," in *Handbook of Positive Psychology*, ed. C. R. Snyder, Erik Wright, and Shane J. Lopez (Oxford: Oxford University Press, 2001), 195–206.

5. I want to acknowledge Arijit Chatterjee for introducing me to the concept of team flow. See Arijit Chatterjee, "Flow in Teams" (paper presented at the meetings of the Academy of Management, Honolulu, 2005) for his insights on this. Arijit and I also wrote a working paper based on his conference paper (and 80 percent Arjit's work) titled "Maintaining the Flow: A Process Model of Over-Performing Teams," which remains unpublished, since both of us shifted to other professional interests, but which I will share upon request.

6. For a good overview of anchoring research, see Daniel Kahneman's chapter 11, "Anchoring" in *Thinking, Slow and Fast* (New York: Farrar, Straus, and Giroux, 2011), 119–28.

7. André L. Delbecq and Andrew H. Van de Ven, "A Group Process Model for Problem Identification and Program Planning," *Journal of Applied Behavioral Science* 7 (July/August, 1971): 466–91. The nominal group technique is a great example of a management technique that has been around for so long that is it easy to forget how valuable it is. There is definitely a bias among MBA and executive education students to discount ideas that are more than ten years old. It is not like group decision-making is a new problem!

8. Paul B. Paulus and Huei-Chuan Yang, "Idea Generation in Groups: A Basis for Creativity in Organizations," *Organizational Behavior and Human Decision Processes* 82, no. 1 (2000): 76–87.

9. Again, like most things related to group decision-making, this is not a new idea, but it is one that I have used effectively over the years. See Jean M. Bartunek and J. Kenneth Murnighan, "The Nominal Group Technique: Expanding the Basic Procedure and Underlying Assumptions," *Group and Organization Studies* 9, no. 3 (1984): 417–32.

10. Brian Mullen, Craig Johnson, and Eduardo Salas, "Productivity Loss in Brainstorming Groups: A Meta-Analytic Integration," *Basic and Applied Social Psychology* 12, no. 1 (1991): 3–23.

11. For a helpful description of brainwriting as well as other ideas for generating creative ideas, see Leigh Thompson, *Creative Conspiracy: The New Rules of Breakthrough Collaboration* (Boston: Harvard Business Review Press, 2013).

12. For a useful set of tools to help enter into these conversations and break out of the hidden conflicts, I recommend Steven S. Taylor, *You're a Genius: Using Reflective Practice to Master the Craft of Leadership* (Business Expert Press, 2015).

Chapter 8

1. I have no insight into these situations beyond what is described in news reports. I recognize that in all likelihood these reports are incomplete and do not tell the whole story. I also understand that the news stories reported here may paint an unfair picture of one or more viewpoints. For this reason, I keep my comments limited to what is reported. I use these examples to illustrate common characteristics of situations in which stakeholder interests and reactions are not well anticipated by leaders. The results of these stories suggest that is the case.

2. "Seeking Dean's Firing: Seminary Professors End Up Jobless," *New York Times*, October 1, 2014; "General Theological Seminary Brings Back Professors It Dismissed," *New York Times*, November 7, 2014.

3. Sapna Maheshwari, "One Day's Notice: Wet Seal under Fire for Surprise Layoffs," BuzzFeed, January 6, 2015, http://www.buzzfeed.com/sapna/one-days-notice-wet-seal-under-fire-for-surprise-layoffs.

4. I make a distinction between stakeholder mapping—which is a technique for identifying individuals and groups relevant to a given task, decision, initiative, or organization—and stakeholder theory. Stakeholder theory emerged from Freeman's seminal book, *Strategic Management: A Stakeholder Approach* (1984) and focuses on the question of who matters for a firm. Thus, stakeholder theory primarily deals with firm-level issues, not decision-level issues. For an excellent extension of stakeholder theory examining stakeholder salience, see Ronald K. Mitchell, Bradley R. Agle, and Donna J. Wood, "Toward a Theory of Stakeholder Identification and Salience: Defining the Principle of Who and What Really Counts," *Academy of Management Review* 22, no. 4 (1997): 853–86.

5. Mitchell, Agle, and Wood, "Toward a Theory of Stakeholder Identification and Salience," 853-886.

6. Having spent the past eight years wrestling with the seven-point scoring template used in an approach to scenario planning that I've taught numerous times, I've learned my lesson.

7. For a good example of frames having implications for the motivation change champions, see this study of LGBT workplace activists. Certain arguments for domestic-partner benefits (namely, that the benefits don't cost much) would have been highly persuasive for the target executives but would have been destructive to the morale of the change team (because they shift the argument away from equality and fairness and to one of simple cost. The implication is that as long as the fix is cheap, the company should not discriminate.). W. E. Douglas Creed, Maureen M. Scully, and John R. Austin,

"Clothes Make the Person? The Tailoring of Legitimating Accounts and the Social Construction of Identity," *Organization Science* 13, no. 5 (2002): 475–96.

8. I place the selected player in the "position known" category because a specific player had not been identified yet, but Rickey was confident he could find a player who shared Rickey's vision for the Dodgers. The African-American community in Brooklyn is in the unknown category, simply because no one from the Dodger organization had reached out to that community yet. Any guess about community support would be based on untested assumptions.

Chapter 9

1. This quote is actually a widely described interpretation of what Heraclitus said, since none of Heraclitus's original writing survives. Plato attributes a similar river image to Heraclitus. Heraclitus is connected with the general idea of nature as being naturally in a state of flux and change.

2. Professor Richard Nielsen introduced me to the Woolman "I am We" method of social engagement in graduate school. I am grateful for that because it has become an anchoring concept throughout my career as a facilitator and educator. I do not engage another person in conversation unless I can sincerely find something I have in common with him or her. I also try to approach the conversation with an attitude of friendliness. If I cannot do both of these things, I will not engage that person. Richard P. Nielsen, "Woolman's 'I am We' Triple-Loop Action Learning: Origin and Application in Organization Ethics," *Journal of Applied Behavioral Science* 29 (1993): 117–38.

Chapter 10

1. W. Hart et al., "Feeling Validated Versus Being Correct: A Meta-Analysis of Selective Exposure to Information," *Psychological Bulletin* 135, no. 4 (2009): 555–88.

2. Frances Frei and Anne Morriss, *Uncommon Service: How to Win by Putting Customers at the Core of Your Business* (Boston: Harvard Business Press, 2012).

3. Sandy Kristin Piderit, "Rethinking Resistance and Recognizing Ambivalence: A Multidimensional View of Attitudes toward an Organizational Change," *Academy of Management Review* 25, no. 4 (2000): 783–94.

4. Paul C. Nutt, "Search during Decision Making," *European Journal of Operational Research* 160 (2005): 851–76.

Chapter 11

1. S. Beechler and Mansour Javidan, "Leading with a Global Mindset," in *Advances in International Management* (Vol. 19), ed. Mansour Javidan, Michael A. Hitt, and R. M. Steers, *The Global Mindset* (New York: Elsevier, 2007).

2. For an in-depth examination of the components of global mindset as well as a comprehensive listing of exercises and resources for developing these attributes, see Mansour Javidan and Jennie L. Walker, *Developing*

Your Global Mindset: The Handbook for Successful Global Leaders (Edina, MN: Beaver's Pond Press, 2013).

3. Tversky and Kahneman described illusory correlation as a form of availability bias in which two things are easy to recall together given their temporal closeness or frequency of occurrence. Amos Tversky and Daniel Kahneman, "Availability: A Heuristic for Judging Frequency and Probability," *Cognitive Psychology* 5, no. 2 (1973): 207–32.

4. Obviously, if there are only two variables involved, it may be possible to observe with some level of confidence, but few of our social problems have only two variables. Our need to infer causation forms a cornerstone of the development of science and philosophy going back at least to Hume's *A Treatise of Human Nature*, published in 1739.

5. Itxaso Barberia et al., "Implementation and Assessment of an Intervention to Debias Adolescents against Causal Illusions," *PLoS ONE* 8, no. 8 (2013): e71303.

6. Dan M. Kahan, "Ideology, Motivated Reasoning, and Cognitive Reflection: An Experimental Study," *Judgment and Decision Making* 8 (2013): 407–24. Dan M. Kahan et al., "The Polarizing Impact of Science Literacy and Numeracy on Perceived Climate Change Risks," *Nature Climate Change* 2 (2012): 732–35.

7. Every industry has these strongly held belief systems. Give it some time, and I am sure you can identify one or two in your own industry. Here are some of the stronger ones I have encountered: there will always be a positive cost-benefit argument in favor of using approved medicines (pharmaceutical industry); regulation always reduces effective economic growth (financial services industry).

8. Eddy J. Davelaar et al., "The Demise of Short-Term Memory Revisited: Empirical and Computational Investigations of Recency Effects," *Psychological Review* 112 (2005): 3–42.

9. Mathew S. Isaac and Robert M. Schindler, "The Top –Ten Effect: Consumers' Subjective Categorization of Ranked Lists," *Journal of Consumer Research* 40, no. 6 (2014): 1181-1202. One interesting finding is that being ranked 10th is far better than being ranked 11th but being ranked 9th or 8th may not really be much better than being ranked 10th

10. Gary Klein, "Performing a Project Premortem," *Harvard Business Review* 85, no. 9 (2007): 18–19.

11. Paul J. H. Schoemaker and Robert. E. Gunther, *Profiting from Uncertainty: Strategies for Succeeding No Matter What the Future Brings* (New York, London: Free Press, 2002).

12. Mae Anderson, "Cheap Razor Made after P&G Watches Indians Shave," Associated Press, Yahoo Finance, October 3, 2013.

13. I thank my former student, Amy Chancellor, for pointing me to Lisa Bodell's book just weeks before this book went to print. It is a great companion book to this one. See Lisa Bodell, *Kill the Company: End the Status Quo, Start an Innovation Revolution* (Bibliomotion, 2012).

Chapter 12

1. An earlier version of this chapter was published in John R. Austin, "Initiating Controversial Strategic Change in Organizations,"

OD Practitioner 41, no. 3 (2009): 24–29. I've made modifications to the original article to align with the unquestioned brilliance theme.

    2. John R. Austin, "A Method for Facilitating Controversial Social Change in Organizations: Branch Rickey and the Brooklyn Dodgers," *Journal of Applied Behavioral Science* 33, no. 1 (1997): 101–18.

    3. Albert Rothenberg, *Emerging Goddess: Creative Process in Art, Science and Other Fields* (Chicago: University of Chicago Press, 1979).

    4. E. F. Schumacher, *A Guide for the Perplexed* (New York: Harper & Row, 1977).

    5. This story is told by David R. Roediger, "Gaining a Hearing for Black-White Unity: Covington Hall and the Complexities of Race, Gender and Class," in *Towards the Abolition of Whiteness : Essays on Race, Politics, and Working Class History* (London, New York: Verso Books, 1994): 127–80.

    6. Robert Kegan, *The Evolving Self: Problem and Process in Human Development* (Cambridge, MA: Harvard University Press, 1982).

    7. Creed, Scully, and Austin, "Clothes Make the Person?" 475–96.

Chapter 13

    1. Jeffrey Pfeffer and Robert I. Sutton, *The Knowing-Doing Gap: How Smart Companies Turn Knowledge into Action* (Boston: Harvard Business School Press, 2000).

    2. Donald Sull and Kathleen M. Eisenhardt, Simple Rules: How to Thrive in a Complex World (Boston: Houghton Mifflin Harcourt, 2015).

    3. Karl E. Weick, "Drop Your Tools: An Allegory for Organizational Studies," *Administrative Science Quarterly* 41, no. 2 (1996): 301–13. There have been many debates in organization theory circles about this account, specifically about the interpretive frame Weick uses to draw his conclusions as well as the implication from the title that Weick is suggesting that we throw out all our skills (our tools) when faced with disaster. The first debate is a useful one to have as a healthy critique of research methods. The second one is a bit of a red herring, since Weick's point is not about forgetting your training when faced with the unfamiliar but rather to recognize when it is time to actually use that training (deploying personal shelters) that is not routine.

    4. Peter M. Senge, *The Fifth Discipline* (New York: Doubleday/Currency, 1990).

Acknowledgments

It takes a certain level of confidence to write a book and a whole lot of people willing to balance encouragement with doses of reality. Students, executive education participants, clients, friends and colleagues have provided both to me over the years. My thinking has evolved through these interactions with individuals too numerous to name.

My interest in overconfidence and cognitive processing has been with me since my time as an undergraduate at Johns Hopkins University but it was my time as a PhD student at Boston College that enabled me to develop my interest in organizational change and strategic thinking. BC faculty and my fellow graduate students taught me the value of questioning dominant mindsets and for that I am grateful. I am indebted to Jean Bartunek for inviting me to co-author a book chapter with her in 2001. That chapter triggered my interest in idea translation and, more significantly, sparked my desire to train leaders to be skilled idea translators.

My time working at Decision Strategies International (DSI) was instrumental in helping me better understand the challenges of strategic thinking and also learn how to challenge leaders to embrace and thrive in uncertain environments. I thank DSI founder Paul Shoemaker for providing the foundation and intellectual guidance that has benefited so many DSI clients over the years. The techniques in part II of this book are certainly stronger due to my time at DSI. Jim Austin, Samantha Howland, Roch Parayre, Kathy Pearson, and the late Franck Schuurmans taught me things I didn't even know I didn't know about how to get successful leaders to think differently. I cannot acknowledge all of my former DSI colleagues but I learned from every member of the DSI team.

A number of people over the past two years allowed me to test and refine the techniques in this book within their organizations and graduate classes. Their time and willingness to experiment helped me create more practical techniques and discover a few dead ends early in the process. I want to specifically thank Deborah Coolidge, Andrew Llewellyn, Angela Taylor, and Tim O'Leary for their help in this regard.

Turning a rough manuscript into a completed book would not have been possible without the editorial advice of Laura Reed-Morrisson and several copy editors. Matthew Williams provided a professional touch with his interior and cover design skills. Laura Waldhier inspires with her photography and I appreciate her help.

Finally, none of this would have been possible without the patience of Caitlin and Patrick Osborne who kept me going with their awesomeness and politely endured those times when my mind was absorbed in my writing.

About the Author

John Austin, photo by
Laura Waldhier

John Austin works at the intersection of research and practice as the president of Three Translation Leadership. Prior to that, Dr. Austin was a principal at Decision Strategies International and on the faculty at Penn State University and the University of Washington, Bothell. He continues to teach executives for the Aresty Institute of Executive Education at The Wharton School (University of Pennsylvania), Georgetown University McDonough School of Business, and the University of North Carolina Kenan-Flagler Business School. Dr. Austin has worked with numerous global Fortune 500 companies and government agencies as an executive development resource.

Dr. Austin has a BA in economics from the Johns Hopkins University and a PhD in organization studies from Boston College. He is a thought leader in the areas of team leadership, organizational change implementation, and strategic decision-making. Dr. Austin's work on knowledge transfer in managerial teams has been used to develop executive teams around the world.

Dr. Austin's research has been published in leading management and applied psychology journals including *Journal of Applied Behavioral Science*, *Journal of Applied Psychology*, *Journal of Organization Design*, and *Organization Science* as well as practice-oriented publications including *HR Magazine* and *OD Practitioner*. His work has been recognized with three Best Paper awards from the Academy of Management and has been mentioned in a number of media outlets. He is the author of *Leading Effective Change: A Primer for the HR Professional*, published as part of the SHRM Foundation's Effective Practice Guidelines Series.

For further information or to contact Dr. Austin, go to www.ThreeTranslationLeadership.com. He is available for training, facilitation, and speaking engagements.